سَميرٌ وَبِنْطالُهُ البُنِّيُّ

حبيب ياغي

Samir and His Brown Trousers

An Elementary-Level
Modern Standard Arabic Reader

by Habeeb Yaghy

© 2023 by Habeeb Yaghy and Matthew Aldrich

The author's moral rights have been asserted. All rights reserved. No part of this document may be reproduced or transmitted in any form or by any means, electronic, mechanical, photocopying, recording, or otherwise, without prior written permission of the publisher.

ISBN: 978-1-949650-89-1

Written by Habeeb Yaghy

Edited by Habeeb Yaghy and Matthew Aldrich

English translation by Habeeb Yaghy and Matthew Aldrich

Cover art by Duc-Minh Vu

Audio by Raghida Abillamaa

website: www.lingualism.com

email: contact@lingualism.com

Table of Contents

Introduction ii

Before Reading (Pre-reading Questions) 1

Prologue 3

The Story 4

Comprehension Questions 44

    Answers 74

Discussion Questions 50

True, False, or Unknown 54

    Answers 84

Fill in the Blank with the Appropriate Verb 60

    Answers 88

Fill in the Blank with the Appropriate Expression 68

    Answers 90

Glossary 92

    Nouns 92

    Adjectives 95

    Verbs 96

    Other 97

Introduction

In *Samir and His Brown Trousers*, Habeeb Yaghy draws Samir as one child among many children worldwide that have likes and dislikes, desires, fears, and secrets but whose parents–overprotective ones in particular–fail to provide them the choice to explore their personalities.

Habeeb Yaghy is certain that his readers–basically, learners of Arabic as a foreign language–will enjoy the story while improving their Arabic language skills and learning about Lebanon's cultural context vividly addressed inside the book.

Before you dive into the story, you are encouraged to answer (or at least think about) the pre-reading questions (p. 2) and study the glossary (p. 92-97) to prepare yourself and make the reading experience more enjoyable.

Each page in Arabic is followed by its English translation, so that you can easily find the equivalents of unknown words and phrases or challenging sentences.

Post-reading activities will help you check your understanding and actively use vocabulary and expressions from the story.

You can make use of the accompanying audio track in a number of ways, depending on your learning preferences and needs. Listen as you follow along silently while reading the text, shadow the narrator to improve your pronunciation and intonation, or listen again (hours, days, weeks) after reading to see how much you can understand.

Visit **www.lingualism.com/audio**, where you can find the **free accompanying audio** to download or stream (at variable playback rates)

This book is also available in Levantine Arabic at www.lingualism.com.

أَسْئِلَةُ ما قَبْلَ القِراءَةِ

اُنْظُروا إِلى صورَةِ غِلافِ الكِتابِ.

مَنْ في الصّورَةِ؟

أَيْنَ هُما؟

ماذا يَفْعَلانِ هُناكَ؟

في أَيِّ فَصْلٍ مِنَ السَّنَةِ هَذِهِ الصّورَةُ؟

اِسْمُ القِصَّةِ "سَميرٌ وَبِنْطالُهُ البُنِّيُّ".

في رَأْيِكُمْ، مَنْ هُوَ سَميرٌ؟

هَلْ هُوَ وَلَدٌ سَعيدٌ؟ لِمَ نَعَمْ أَوْ لِمَ لا؟

هَلْ هَذِهِ المَلابِسُ جَميلَةٌ؟

هَلْ تُحِبّونَ أَلْوانَ ثِيابِ الوَلَدِ؟

في رَأْيِكُمْ، هَلْ يُحِبُّ سَميرٌ بِنْطالَهُ؟

Before Reading

Look at the book cover.

    Who is in the picture?

    Where are they?

    What are they doing there?

    In what season of the year is this picture?

The story title is "Samir and His Brown Trousers."

    In your opinion, who is Samir?

    Is he a happy boy? Why?

    Are these clothes nice?

    Do you like the colors of the boy's clothes?

    In your opinion, does Samir like his trousers?

Prologue

It is the first month of the year, and Beirut is witnessing stormy weather associated with dense clouds and strong and cold winds. In such terrible weather, people in the capital of Lebanon normally throw on heavy wool clothes, usually dark in color, as one way of staying warm. And in a small family living close to downtown Beirut, a little boy's mother worries about her only little child, Samir, being cold at school. To keep Samir warm, *Umm Samir* (Samir's mother), together with her husband, gets involved in the boy's decision by making him pick her plan. This will bring the boy sadness that starts at home and continues inside the classroom.

Samir, now a grandfather, goes back in time to that January day while waiting for dinner at his son's home. He can never forget the grief and disappointment he experienced in the class of Arabic language that day. He recounts what happens at school to Adel and Maya, the two grandchildren who enjoy the fun story.

سَميرٌ وَبِنْطالُهُ البُنِّيُّ

يَروي سَميرٌ لِحَفيدَيهِ عَنْ ذَلِكَ اليَوْمِ مِنْ أَيّامِ شَهْرِ يَنايَرَ. كانَ في الصَّفِّ الثّالِثِ الإبْتِدائِيِّ في مَدْرَسَةٍ لِلرُّهْبانِ،[1] وَكانَتِ المَدْرَسَةُ في وَسَطِ مَدينَةِ بَيْروتَ.

ذَلِكَ اليَوْمُ كانَ مُمْطِرًا وَكانَ فيهِ ريحٌ شَديدَةٌ. الجَوُّ كانَ بارِدًا جِدًّا. حَرارَتُهُ تِسْعُ دَرَجاتٍ. وَفي السَّماءِ غُيومٌ سَوْداءُ كانَ الهَواءُ يَلْعَبُ بِها يَمينًا وَيَسارًا، يَرْفَعُها إلى فَوْقُ ثُمَّ يَرْميها إلى تَحْتُ. يَوْمٌ مِثْلُ هَذا مِنْ أَيّامِ الشِّتاءِ في بَيْروتَ هُوَ يَوْمٌ رَمادِيٌّ. يَوْمٌ مِثْلُ هَذا هُوَ يَوْمٌ حَزينٌ.

هُوَ أَيْضًا كانَ حَزينًا. كُلَّ صَباحٍ كانَ يَحْمِلُ شَنْطَتَهُ وَيَخْرُجُ مِنَ المَنْزِلِ في السّاعَةِ السّادِسَةِ والنِّصْفِ وَيَنْتَظِرُ باصَ المَدْرَسَةِ في الشّارِعِ.

لَكِنْ في ذَلِكَ الصَّباحِ، ما كانَ وَحْدَهُ. كانَتْ أُمُّهُ تَقِفُ بِجانِبِهِ في الشّارِعِ. هُوَ كانَ يَلْبَسُ مِعْطَفَهُ وَيَضَعُ قُبَّعَةً مِنَ الصّوفِ، وَهِيَ تَلْبَسُ رِداءً مِنَ الصّوفِ لَكِنْ لا تَضَعُ قُبَّعَةً.

Samir is telling his two grandchildren about a January day. He was in the third grade of elementary school. The school was run by monks[1] and was located in downtown Beirut.

That day was rainy and very windy. The weather was very cold. The temperature was nine degrees. There were black clouds in the sky with which the air played left and right, lifting them up and then throwing them down. A day like this in Beirut is a gray day. A day like this is a sad day.

He, too, was sad. Every morning he would pick up his bag, leave the house at half past six, and wait for the school bus on the street.

But that morning, he was not alone. His mother was standing next to him on the street. He was wearing his coat and a wool hat, and she was wearing a wool robe but no hat.

---

[1] Private education in Lebanon is mostly dependent on religious institutions, among which are the Catholic schools, whose foundation dates back to the 17th century and which offer high-level academics with students learning in three languages: Arabic, French, and English.

حاوَلَتْ أُمُّهُ أَنْ تَرْويَ لَهُ قِصَصًا مُضْحِكَةً لِأَنَّهُ ما كانَ سَعيدًا. هِيَ تَعْرِفُ لِماذا ابْنُها حَزينٌ. وَقَفَتْ مَعَهُ نِصْفَ ساعَةٍ حَتّى وَصَلَ الباصُ.

"قُبْلَةٌ. قُبْلَتانِ. وَهَذِهِ ثَلاثُ قُبْلاتٍ يا حَبيبي. هَيّا! ابْتَسِمْ يا ابْني ... مَعَ السَّلامَةِ."[1]

وَهُوَ بِصَوْتٍ حَزينٍ أجابَ "مَعَ السَّلامَةِ" وَرَكِبَ الباصَ.

بِخَجَلٍ قالَ لِسائِقِ الباصِ "صَباحُ الخَيْرِ" وَذَهَبَ إلى المَقْعَدِ الخَلْفيِّ. هُناكَ لا يَجْلِسُ التَّلاميذُ.

خَلَعَ مِعْطَفَهُ وَوَضَعَهُ عَلى المَقْعَدِ. خَلَعَ قُبَّعَتَهُ وَوَضَعَها فَوْقَ المِعْطَفِ. نَظَرَ إلى مَلابِسِهِ. نَظَرَ إلى بِنْطالِهِ. نَظَرَ إِلَيْهِ كَثيرًا. ثُمَّ قالَ لِنَفْسِهِ: "أنا في هَذِهِ المَلابِسِ مِثْلُ شَجَرَةٍ"!

"اِسْمَعا القِصَّةَ يا صَغيرَيَّ." قالَ سَميرٌ.

"ما هِيَ القِصَّةُ يا جَدّي؟" سَأَلَ الوَلَدُ الصَّغيرُ.

"عَنْ أيَّةِ قِصَّةٍ تُريدُ أنْ تَتَكَلَّمَ يا جَدّي؟" سَأَلَتِ البِنْتُ الصَّغيرَةُ.

His mother tried to tell him funny stories because he wasn't happy. She knew why her son was sad. She stood with him for half an hour until the bus arrived.

"This is a kiss for you. These are two kisses for you. And these are three kisses, my love. Come on, smile, my son… bye!"[1]

In a sad voice, he answered, "Bye-bye," and got on the bus.

He shyly said to the bus driver, "Good morning," and went to the back seat. There, not a single student was sitting.

He took off his coat and put it on the bench. He took off his hat and put it on over the coat. He looked at his clothes. He looked at his trousers. He looked at the trousers a lot. Then he said to himself, "I look like a tree in these clothes!"

"Listen to the story, my little ones," Samir said.

"What's the story, Grandpa?" asked the little boy.

"What story do you want to tell, Grandpa?" asked the little girl.

---

[1] In Lebanon, it is common to kiss three times on alternating cheeks, with the other person's left cheek kissed first.

كانَ الوَلَدانِ يَجْلِسانِ عَلى أريكَةِ¹ البَهْوِ² الكَبيرَةِ بِجانِبِ جَدِّهِما، كُلُّ واحِدٍ عَلى جِهَةٍ. ذَلِكَ اليَوْمُ كانَ أيْضًا يَوْمًا مِنْ أيّامِ يَنايِرَ. كانَتِ السّاعَةُ الثّامِنَةَ والنِّصْفَ لَيْلًا، أيْ قَبْلَ وَقْتِ العَشاءِ بِنِصْفِ ساعَةٍ.

"رُبَّما كُنْتُ في عُمرِكَ أنْتَ يا عادِلُ. كَمْ عُمرُكُما الآنَ يا عادِلُ وَيا مايا؟"

"أنا عُمري ثَماني سَنَواتٍ وَشَهْرانِ يا جَدّي." أجابَ عادِلٌ بِاللُّغَةِ الفَرَنْسِيَّةِ. وَعادِلٌ وَلَدٌ لَيْسَ سَمينًا وَلَيْسَ نَحيلًا. هُوَ أشْقَرُ وَعَيْناهُ زَرْقاوانِ وَكَبيرَتانِ.

"وَأنْتِ يا مايا؟ كَمْ عُمْرُكِ؟" سَألَ سَميرٌ حَفيدَتَهُ.

"عُمري سِتُّ سَنَواتٍ وَ ... مْمْمْ: واحِدٌ، اِثْنانِ، ثَلاثَةٌ، ...، سِتَّةٌ، ... سِتُّ سَنَواتٍ وَسَبْعَةُ أشْهُرٍ يا جَدّي." قالَتِ البِنْتُ بِاللُّغَةِ الفَرَنْسِيَّةِ أيْضًا. وَمايا بِنْتٌ نَحيلَةٌ جِدًّا. هِيَ شَقْراءُ مِثْلُ عادِلٍ وَشَعْرُها طَويلٌ وَأمْلَسُ وَلَكِنْ عَيْناها بُنِّيَّتانِ.

"وَأنا كُنْتُ في السّابِعَةِ مِنْ عُمْري. كانَ عُمْري بَيْنَ عُمْرِكَ يا عادِلُ وَعُمْرِكِ يا مايا. وَكُنْتُ في الصَّفِّ الثّالِثِ الإبْتِدائِيِّ. نادَتِ المُعَلِّمَةُ أمينًا: يا أمينُ. تَفَضَّلْ إلى السَّبّورَةِ واكْتُبِ الكَلِماتِ الأرْبَعَ. وَأمينٌ ..."

The two children were sitting on the large sofa[1] in the parlor[2] next to their grandfather, each on one side. That day was also a January day. It was half past eight at night, half an hour before dinner time.

"Perhaps I was your age, Adel. How old are you now, Adel and Maya?"

"I am eight years and two months old, Grandpa," Adel replied in French. Adel is neither fat nor skinny. He is blond, and his eyes are blue and big.

"And you, Maya? How old are you?" Samir asked his granddaughter.

"I am six years old and… mmm: one, two, three, …, six, … six years and seven months, Grandpa." The girl said in French, too. Maya is a very skinny girl. She is blonde like Adel, with long, straight hair, but her eyes are brown.

"And I was seven years old. My age was between your age, Adel, and yours, Maya. I was in the third grade of elementary school. The teacher called on Amin: 'Amin, go to the board and write the four words. And Amin…"

---

[1] أَرِيكَةٌ (sofa) and صوفا (couch), a word you'll meet later in the story, are, like their English translations, technically synonymous and interchangeable, but أَرِيكَةٌ (sofa) tends to be used for a more formal, nice piece of furniture, while صوفا (couch) brings to mind a more casual, comfy piece of furniture you can lay back on and watch TV.

[2] بَهْوٌ (parlor) is a formal sitting room for entertaining guests, as opposed to غُرْفَةُ جُلوسٍ (living room), which is a more casual room for daily relaxing and watching TV.

"مَنْ هُوَ أمينٌ يا جَدّي؟" سَأَلَ عادِلٌ.

"هُوَ تِلْميذٌ ذَكِيٌّ وَدائِمًا يَفْعَلُ كُلَّ واجِباتِهِ. دَفْتَرُهُ مُرَتَّبٌ، وَخَطُّهُ جَميلٌ جِدًّا. سارَ أمينٌ إلى السَّبّورَةِ، وَكَتَبَ الكَلِماتِ. كَلِماتٌ جَديدَةٌ وَفيها التّاءُ المَبْسوطَةُ والتّاءُ المَرْبوطَةُ!"[1]

"وَكَيْفَ كانَتِ المُعَلِّمَةُ؟ هَلْ كانَتْ لَطيفَةً؟" سَأَلَتْ مايا.

"نَعَمْ، نَعَمْ. كانَتْ لَطيفَةً جِدًّا مَعَ الأَوْلادِ. وَكانَتْ جَميلَةً جِدًّا: عَيْناها خَضْراوانِ، وَفَمُها زَهْرِيٌّ، وَشَعْرُها أَسْوَدُ وَأَمْلَسُ. تَشْرَحُ لَنا دُروسًا سَهْلَةً وَتَقولُ النُّكَتَ وَ..."

"أنا أُحِبُّ المُعَلِّمَةَ اللَّطيفَةَ. مُعَلِّمَةُ اللُّغَةِ العَرَبِيَّةِ في مَدْرَسَتِنا أَحْيانًا تَغْضَبُ عَلى التِّلْميذِ الكَسولِ، وَعِدَّةَ مَرّاتٍ نَخافُ مِنْها."

مايا قالَتْ: "لا يا عادِلُ. مَدامْ زينَةَ صَديقَتي. هِيَ لَطيفَةٌ وَتُحِبُّني! يا جَدّي، هَلْ كَتَبَ ... ما اسْمُهُ ... نَعَمْ، أمينٌ ... هَلْ كَتَبَ أمينٌ الكَلِماتِ الأَرْبَعَ جَيِّدًا جِدًّا؟"

"Who is Amin, Grandpa?" Adel asked.

"He is a smart student and always does all his homework. His notebook is neat, and his handwriting is very beautiful. Amin walked to the board and wrote the words. They were new words that contained the "ta' mabsoutah" and the "ta' marboutah!"[1]

"And how was the teacher? Was she nice?" Maya asked.

"Yes, yes. She was very nice to the students. And she was very pretty; her eyes were green, her mouth pink, and her hair black and straight. She used to explain to us easy lessons, tell jokes, and..."

"I love a kind teacher. The Arabic language teacher in our school sometimes gets angry at a lazy student, and we are often afraid of her."

Maya said, "No, Adel. Mrs. Zeina is my friend. She is sweet and loves me! Grandpa, did he write... What's his name... Yes, Amin... Did Amin write the four words very well?"

---

[1] The name of the letter ت is تاءٌ (ta'). It is referred to as تاءٌ مَبْسُوطَةٌ (ta' mabsoutah), literally, 'happy T,' to distinguish it from the variant form ة, which is called تاءٌ مَرْبوطَةٌ (ta' marboutah), literally 'tied T," so named because its ends are 'tied' together to form a loop.

"لا. أمينٌ ما كَتَبَ الكَلِماتِ جَيِّدًا جِدًّا. كانَ عِنْدَهُ أخْطاءٌ. قالَتْ لَهُ المُعَلِّمَةُ: اِسْمَعْ يا أمينُ: الكَلِمَةُ الأولى سَهْلَةٌ وَهِيَ فِعْلٌ. وَالكَلِمَةُ الثّانِيَةُ سَهْلَةٌ وَهِيَ فِعْلٌ أيْضًا. لكِنِ الكَلِمَةُ الثّالِثَةُ اسْمٌ. وَالكَلِمَةُ الرّابِعَةُ صِفَةٌ.'

أرادَتْ أنْ تُساعِدَهُ أكْثَرَ مِنْ مَرَّةٍ، فقالَتْ في الأخيرِ: 'التّاءُ في الكَلِمَةِ الصِّفَةِ بَرْدانَةٌ هِيَ حَقّاً بَرْدانَةٌ. لِماذا؟ لِأنَّ يَدَها اليُسْرى لا تَتْرُكُ يَدَها اليُمْنى. لكِنِ التّاءُ في الكَلِمَةِ الفِعْلِ لَيْسَتْ بَرْدانَةً.'[1]

أمينٌ ما فَهِمَ. وَبَعْدَ دَقيقَةٍ، اِبْتَسَمَتِ المُعَلِّمَةُ وَقالَتْ: 'لا بَأْسَ يا أمينُ. في المَرَّةِ المُقْبِلَةِ سَوْفَ تَكْتُبُ مِنْ دونِ أخْطاءٍ، أنا أعْرِفُ. شُكْرًا لَكَ. عُدْ إلى مَكانِكَ، مِنْ فَضْلِكَ.'"

"وَماذا قالَ الصَّبِيُّ المِسْكينُ؟" سَأَلَ عادِلٌ جَدَّهُ.

"كانَ أمينٌ تِلْميذًا مُجْتَهِدًا. لا أعْرِفُ لِماذا كَتَبَ الكَلِمَةَ الصِّفَةَ خَطَأً، وَكَتَبَ فِعْلًا مِنَ الفِعْلَيْنِ خَطَأً أيْضًا. عادَ إلى مَقْعَدِهِ وَهُوَ يَبْكي."

سَأَلَ الجَدُّ عادِلًا: "هَلْ تَعْرِفُ هَذا الدَّرْسَ يا عادِلُ؟"

"No. Amin did not write the words very well. He made mistakes. The teacher said to him, 'Listen, Amin. The first word is easy, and it is a verb. The second word is easy too, and it is also a verb. But the third word is a noun. The fourth word is an adjective.'

She wanted to help him more than once, so she finally said, 'The ta' in the adjective word cold is really cold. Why? Because her left hand does not leave her right hand. But the ta' in the verb is not cold.'[1]

Amin didn't understand. After a minute, the teacher smiled at Amin and said: 'It's okay, Amin. Next time, you will write without mistakes, I know. Thank you. Go back to your seat, please.'"

"And what did the poor boy say?" Adel asked his grandfather.

"Amin was a diligent student. I don't know why he wrote the adjective word incorrectly and wrote one of the two verbs incorrectly, as well. He went back to his seat, crying."

Grandpa asked Adel, "Do you know this lesson, Adel?"

---

[1] The teacher is using a mnemonic to help her students understand which ta' to use. She is inferring that ta' marbouta (ة)–literally 'tied ta'–resembles two hands (ends of the line) touching or bound together. Here, the teacher wants Amin to imagine the letter rubbing or wiggling its 'hands' together to create warmth in the cold weather, instead of leaving the two hands apart as in the case of the ت.

"نَعَمْ يا جَدّي. هَذا دَرْسٌ صَعْبٌ وَلا أُحِبُّهُ." أجابَ عادِلٌ.

"هَلْ نَدْرُسُ هَذِهِ التّاءَ وَتِلْكَ التّاءَ نَحْنُ أَيْضًا؟"

"لا. المُعَلِّمَةُ سَوْفَ تَشْرَحُ هَذا الدَّرْسَ في السَّنَةِ المُقْبِلَةِ."

"الحَمْدُ لِلهِ!" أجابَتْ مايا.

"أَكْمِلْ يا جَدّي." قال عادِلٌ.

"نَظَرَ كُلُّ تِلْميذٍ في الصَّفِّ إلى الآخَرِ لِأَنَّ أمينًا عادَةً لا يَفْعَلُ أَخْطاءً في الإمْلاءِ. نادَتْني المُعَلِّمَةُ: 'يا سَميرُ. هَلْ تَعْرِفُ كَيْفَ نَكْتُبُ هَذِهِ الكَلِماتِ؟'

'نَعَمْ، أنا أَعْرِفُ لَكِنّي لا أُريدُ أنْ أذْهَبَ إلى السَّبّورَةِ.'

'لِماذا يا سَميرُ؟ هَلْ ... هَلْ أَنْتَ خائِفٌ؟ أَنْتَ مُجْتَهِدٌ.'

'لا يا آنِسَةُ.'

'هَلْ أَنْتَ مَوْجوعٌ، لا سَمَحَ اللهُ؟'

'لا يا آنِسَةُ.'

'هَلْ أَنْتَ بَرْدانٌ مِثْلُ التّاءِ في الكَلِمَةِ الصِّفَةِ؟'

'ضَحِكَ التَّلاميذُ، وَنَظَروا إلَيَّ. أنا ما ضَحِكْتُ.'

'ما بِكَ يا حَبيبي؟ هَلْ أَنْتَ حَزينٌ قَليلًا اليَوْمَ؟'

"Yes, Grandpa. This is a hard lesson, and I don't like it." Adel replied.

"Do we study this ta' and that ta' too?"

"No. The teacher will explain this lesson next year."

"Praise be to God!" Maya answered.

"Go on, Grandpa," Adel said.

"Every student in the class looked at the other because Amin usually does not make mistakes in spelling. The teacher called on me. 'Samir, do you know how we write these words?'

'Yes, I know, but I don't want to go to the blackboard.'

'Why Samir? Are you... are you afraid? You are hard-working.'

'No, miss.'

'Are you in pain, God forbid?'

'No, miss.'

'Are you cold like the ta' in the adjective word?'

'The students laughed and looked at me. I didn't laugh.'

'What's wrong with you, dear? Are you a little sad today?'

"أَنا أَعْرِفُ الإِجابَةَ، وَلَكِنْ ..."

تابَعَ الجَدُّ وَهُوَ يَضْحَكُ: "ثُمَّ بَكَيْتُ!"

وَبِسُرْعَةٍ سَأَلَ الصَّبِيُّ الصَّغيرُ جَدَّهُ: "ما كانَ بِكَ يا جَدّي؟ لِماذا بَكَيْتَ؟"

والبِنْتُ سَأَلَتْ جَدَّها: "صَحيحٌ، ما كانَتِ المُشْكِلَةُ يا جَدّي؟ هَلْ كانَ هُناك بَرْدٌ في الصَّفِّ؟"

"اِسْمَعا يا عادِلُ وَيا مايا."

وَبَدَأَ سَميرٌ يَرْوي لِحَفيدَيْهِ قِصَّتَهُ عَنْ ذَلِكَ اليَوْمِ الحَزينِ مِنْ أَيَّامِ الشِّتاءِ.

"كانَ لِأَبي ابْنَةُ عَمَّةٍ تَسْكُنُ في مِنْطَقَتِنا، في العاصِمَةِ بَيْروتَ. كانَتْ تَعْمَلُ خَيَّاطَةً في شَقَّتِها الصَّغيرَةِ. تَعْمَلُ كُلَّ اليَوْمِ. تِلْكَ السَّيِّدَةُ، واسْمُها سُعادُ، كانَتْ في السِّتّينِيَّاتِ مِنْ عُمْرِها. لَها شَعْرٌ كَسْتَنائِيٌّ وَمُجَعَّدٌ، وَلَها عَيْنانِ سَوْداوانِ وَصَغيرَتانِ. زَوْجُها، وَهُوَ رَجُلٌ كَبيرٌ في السِّنِّ وَمَريضٌ، ما كانَ عِنْدَهُ وَظيفَةٌ. كانَ يَسْتَلْقي عَلى السَّريرِ كُلَّ اليَوْمِ وَلا يَخْرُجُ مِنَ الغُرْفَةِ. بِالقُرْبِ مِنْهُ، عَلى طاوِلَةٍ صَغيرَةٍ، كانَ هُناك الكَثيرُ مِنْ عُلَبِ الدَّواءِ.

'I know the answer, but…'"

The grandfather continued while laughing, "Then, I cried!"

Quickly, the little boy asked his grandfather, "What was wrong with you, Grandpa? Why did you cry?"

And the girl asked her grandfather, "Right, what was the problem, Grandpa? Was it chilly in the classroom?"

"Listen, Adel and Maya."

And Samir began to tell his two grandchildren the story of that sad winter's day.

"My father had a cousin who lived in our area, in the capital city of Beirut. She used to work as a seamstress in her small apartment. She would work all day. That woman, Souad, was in her sixties. She had brown curly hair and small, dark eyes. Her husband, an old, sick man, did not have a job. He wanted to be in bed all day and did not leave the room. Near him, on a small table, were many medicine boxes.

في يَوْمٍ مِنْ أَيّامِ الشِّتاءِ البارِدَةِ وَأَنا في غُرْفَتي أَكْتُبُ إِنْشاءً بِاللُّغَةِ العَرَبِيَّةِ، سَمِعْتُ والِدَتي تَقولُ:

'عِنْدي فِكْرَةٌ يا زَوْجي. البَرْدُ في كُلِّ مَكانٍ. ما رَأْيُكَ في أَنْ تَذْهَبَ إِلى سُعادَ وَتَأْخُذَ مَعَكَ هَذِهِ القِطْعَةَ مِنَ القُماشِ؟'

'عَنْ أَيَّةِ قِطْعَةٍ مِنَ القُماشِ تَتَكَلَّمينَ يا حَبيبَتي؟'

'عَنْ هَذِهِ. اُنْظُرْ. هِيَ هَدِيَّتُكَ في عيدِ ميلادي قَبْلَ سَنَتَيْنِ. أَلا تَتَذَكَّرُ؟'

'آهٍ، بَلى. بَلى. أَنا أَتَذَكَّرُ الآنَ.'

'فَكَّرْتُ كَثيرًا. ماذا سَتَفْعَلينَ بِها يا أُمَّ سَميرٍ[1]؟ ماذا سَتَفْعَلينَ بِها يا أُمَّ سَميرٍ؟'

'وَماذا سَتَفْعَلينَ بِها يا أُمَّ سَميرٍ؟'

'خِزانَتي فيها الكَثيرُ مِنَ المَلابِسِ. فَما رَأْيُكَ في أَنْ تَأْخُذَ القُماشَةَ إِلى سُعادَ في نِهايَةِ الأُسْبوعِ؟'

'فِكْرَةٌ جَميلَةٌ. لَكِنْ هَلْ آخُذُها إِلى سُعادَ؟! لَيْسَ هُناكَ أَكْثَرُ مِنَ الأَقْمِشَةِ في بَيْتِها.'

On a cold winter's day, while I was in my room writing a composition in Arabic, I heard my mother say:

'I have an idea, my husband. The weather is cold. How about you go to Souad's and take this piece of cloth with you?'

'What piece of cloth are you talking about, my love?'

'About this one. Look. It was your gift for my birthday two years ago. Don't you remember?'

'Oh, yes, yes. I remember now.'

'I thought a lot. What are you going to do with it, Umm Samir?[1] What are you going to do with it, Umm Samir?'

'And what will you do with it, Umm Samir?'

'My closet has a lot of clothes. How about you take the piece of cloth to Souad at the end of the week?'

'That sounds good. But should I take it to Souad?! She already has plenty of cloth at home.'

---

[1] Umm Samir is an example of a teknonym (كُنْيَة in Arabic). A teknonym is a name that is derived from the name of a person's child. For example, the father of Ali would be referred to as Abu Ali, which means "father of Ali". Similarly, the mother of Fatima would be referred to as Umm Fatima, which means "mother of Fatima". Referring to a father or mother as such is a source of honor for them because having a baby boy in the family is considered to be support to the family.

ضَحِكَتْ أُمِّي، وَقالَتْ: 'لا يا حَبيبي. اِسْمَعْ فِكْرَتي. خُذِ القِطْعَةَ وَخُذْ مَعَكَ سَميرًا وَقُلْ لاِبْنَةِ عَمَّتِكَ: زَوْجَتي تَرجو مِنْكِ أَنْ تَصْنَعي مِنْها بِنْطالًا لاِبْنِنا سَمير. وَنَدْفَعُ لَكِ مالًا.'

'مِسْكينَةٌ. سَتَقولُ نَعَم. هِيَ لا تَأْخُذُ مالًا مِنِ ابْنِ خالِها لَكِنّي سَأُساعِدُها بِالمالِ. هِيَ في حاجَةٍ إِلى أَنْ تَشْتَرِيَ الطَّعامَ والأَدْوِيَةَ.'

'هَذا مُمْتازٌ. وَهَلْ زَوْجُها بِخَيْرٍ في هَذِهِ الأَيّامِ؟'

'لَيْسَ كَثيرًا! صِحَّةُ زَوْجِها سَيِّئَةٌ. هُوَ يَتَناوَلُ الكَثيرَ مِنَ الدَّواءِ يَوْمًا بَعْدَ يَوْمٍ.'

'مِسْكينَةٌ سُعاد. هِيَ تَعْمَلُ كُلَّ اليَوْمِ وَزَوْجُها يَنامُ لِأَنَّهُ مَريضٌ وَلا يَخْرُجُ. هُما في حاجَةٍ إِلى المُساعَدَةِ، لا شَكَّ.'

كانَ عادِلٌ ومايا سَعيدَيْنِ بِالقِصَّةِ. كانا يَنْظُرانِ إِلى الرَّجُلِ الكَبيرِ في السِّنِّ الجالِسِ بَيْنَهُما وَهُما يَبْتَسِمانِ كُلَّ الوَقْتِ. ثُمَّ اسْتَلْقى عادِلٌ عَلى الأَريكَةِ، وَوَضَعَ رَأْسَهُ عَلى صَدْرِ جَدِّهِ. أُمُّ عادِلٍ كانَتْ في المَطْبَخِ تُحَضِّرُ العَشاءَ وَتَسْتَمِعُ إِلى القِصَّةِ أَيْضًا.

My mother laughed and said, 'No, my love. Listen to my idea. Take the piece, take Samir with you, and say to your cousin: My wife wishes you would make trousers out of it for our son, Samir. And we'll pay you money.'

'Poor thing. She will say yes. She does not take money from her cousin, but I will help her with money. She needs to buy food and medicine.'

'That's perfect. Is her husband well these days?'

'Not very! Her husband's health is bad. He takes a lot of medicine day in, day out.'

'Poor Souad. She works all day, and her husband sleeps because he is sick and does not go out. They need help, no doubt.'"

Adel and Maya were happy with the story. They were looking at the old man sitting between them, and they were smiling the whole time. Then Adel lay down on the sofa and laid his head on his grandfather's chest. Umm Adel was in the kitchen preparing dinner and listening to the story, too.

وَسَأَلَ سَمِيرٌ الحَفِيدَينِ: "ما رَأْيُكُما بِالفِكْرَةِ؟"

قالَتْ مايا: "الفِكْرَةُ ذَكِيَّةٌ."

ثُمَّ قالَ عادِلٌ: "نَعَمْ، فِكْرَةٌ ذَكِيَّةٌ. سُعادُ تَشْتَري الطَّعامَ أَوِ الدَّواءَ لِزَوْجِها، أَوْ تَشْتَري أَيَّ شَيْءٍ آخَرَ لَها أَوْ لِزَوْجِها أَوْ لِلبَيْتِ."

وَسَأَلَتِ البِنْتُ الجَدَّ: "وَهَلْ ذَهَبْتُما إِلى السَّيِّدَةِ الخَيّاطَةِ؟"

ضَحِكَ سَمِيرٌ. "نَعَمْ، ذَهَبْنا إِلى السَّيِّدَةِ الخَيّاطَةِ في مَساءِ يَوْمِ السَّبْتِ ..."

"كَيْفَ ذَهَبْتُما؟" سَأَلَ الصَّبِيُّ.

"ذَهَبْنا بِسَيّارَةِ أَبي. كانَ عِنْدَهُ سَيّارَةٌ نَذْهَبُ بِها إِلى سُعادَ وَإِلى الجَبَلِ وَإِلى الشّاطِئِ وَإِلى كُلِّ مَكانٍ. وَهوَ يَذْهَبُ بِها إِلى العَمَلِ كُلَّ صَباحٍ، وَيَرْجِعُ بِها إِلى البَيْتِ في المَساءِ."

الوَلَدانِ مَسْرورانِ. يُريدانِ أَنْ يَسْمَعا القِصَّةَ كُلَّها. وَيُريدانِ أَنْ يَعْرِفا كُلَّ شَيْءٍ عَنْ جَدِّهِما.

"أَكْمِلْ لَنا، لَوْ سَمَحْتَ." قالَ عادِلٌ.

"أَيْنَ نَحْنُ الآنَ في القِصَّةِ يا مايا؟"

Samir asked the two grandchildren, "What do you think of the idea?"

"The idea is clever," Maya said.

Then Adel said, "Yes, a smart idea. Souad buys food or medicine for her husband or anything else for herself, her husband, or the house.

And the girl asked the grandfather, "And did you two go to the lady seamstress?"

Samir laughed. "Yes, we went to the lady seamstress on Saturday evening…"

"How did you go?" asked the boy.

"We went in my father's car. He had a car to take us to Souad, the mountain, the beach, and everywhere. He goes to work every morning by car and returns home in the evening by car, too."

The two children are delighted. They want to hear the whole story. They want to know everything about their grandfather.

"Go on, please," Adel said.

"Where are we now in the story, Maya?"

"القِصَّةُ جَمِيلَةٌ. نَحْنُ في ... نَحْنُ في ..."

بِسُرْعَةٍ أجابَ عادِلٌ: "أنا أعْرِفُ. ذَهَبْتُما إلى سُعادَ في يَوْمِ السَّبْتِ."

"عَظِيمٌ! أخْرَجَتْ سُعادُ تِلْكَ القِطعَةَ مِنَ الكِيسِ وَأنا نَظَرْتُ إلى القِطعَةِ. ما هَذا اللَّوْنَ؟ بُنِّيٌّ؟ لِماذا تُرِيدُ أُمِّي هَذا اللَّوْنَ لي؟ وَمَن قال لِأُمِّي وَأبي إنِّي أُرِيدُ بِنْطالًا بُنِّيًّا؟

طَلَبَتْ مِنِّي سُعادُ أنْ أقِفَ أمامَها لِتَأخُذَ مَقاسي. ثُمَّ قالَتْ: 'سَيَكُونُ جاهِزًا بَعْدَ يَوْمَيْنِ يا صَغِيري. اليَوْمُ هُوَ يَوْمُ السَّبْتِ. غَدًا هُوَ يَوْمُ الأحَدِ. بَعْدَ غَدٍ سَيَكُونُ بِنْطالُكَ جاهِزًا.'

وَنَظَرَتْ إلى أبي، وَأكْمَلَتْ: 'مِسكِينٌ هُوَ سَمِيرٌ يا ابْنَ خالي. يَشْعُرُ بِالبَرْدِ في المَدْرَسَةِ، لا شَكَّ.'

وَسَألَتْني وَفَمُها فَوْقَ أُذُني: 'هَلْ تَشْعُرُ بِالبَرْدِ في المَدْرَسَةِ يا عُمْري؟'

قُلْتُ: 'نَعَم، مَرّاتٍ ... لا، لا، أبَدًا. الصَّفُ فيهِ تَدْفِئَةٌ. لا أظُنُّ أنّي في حاجَةٍ إلى بِنْطالٍ آخَرَ لِلشِّتاءِ. عِنْدي الكَثيرُ مِنَ البَناطيلِ في الخِزانَةِ.'

"The story is beautiful. We are in... We are in..."

Adel answered quickly, "I know! You went to Souad's on Saturday."

"Great! Souad took that piece of cloth out of the bag, and I looked at the piece. What is this color? Brown? Why does my mom want this color for me? And who told my mom and dad that I wanted brown trousers?

Souad asked me to stand in front of her to take my size. Then she said, 'It will be ready in two days, my child. Today is Saturday. Tomorrow is Sunday. The day after tomorrow, your trousers will be ready.'

And she looked at my father and continued, 'Poor Samir, my cousin. He's cold at school, no doubt.'

And she asked me with her mouth above my ear, 'Do you feel cold in school, my life?'

I said, 'Yes, several times... No, no, never! The classroom is heated. I don't think I need another pair of trousers for the winter. I have a lot of trousers in the closet.'

فَقالَتْ: "لَكِنْ هَذا أَطْرى شوز."

مايا فَهِمَتِ العِبارَةَ وَضَحِكَتْ. "كَمْ هِيَ مُضْحِكَةٌ سُعادُ." قالَتْ مايا سَعيدَةً.

"وَما مَعْنى هَذا يا مايا؟" سَأَلَ أَخوها.

"الْمَرْأَةُ تَعْني بِالْفَرَنْسِيَّةِ autre chose."[1]

ضَحِكَ عادِلٌ أَيْضًا، ثُمَّ قالَ: "خَيّاطَةٌ مُضْحِكَةٌ."

هُنا قالَتْ مايا: "هَؤُلاءِ النّاسُ، مِثْلُ تانْتْ سُعادَ وَمَدام زينة، أَذْكِياءُ."

"نَعَمْ يا حُلْوَتي، سُعادُ سَيِّدَةٌ ذَكِيَّةٌ وَتُحِبُّ النّاسَ الأَذْكِياءَ أَيْضًا. وَذَوْقُها في الخِياطَةِ جَميلٌ. الكُلُّ يُحِبُّ ذَوْقَها. تَعَلَّمَتِ الخِياطَةَ في عُمْرٍ صَغيرٍ في حَيٍّ مِنْ أَحْياءِ بَيروتَ القَديمَةِ، وَكانَ عِنْدَها زَبوناتٌ في بَيْروتَ وَفي مُدُنٍ أُخْرى. كانَ عِنْدَها زَبوناتٌ في القُرى أَيْضًا.

كانَتْ تُحَضِّرُ لي الشّوكولاتَةَ بِالحَليبِ أَوِ الكاكاوَ بِالحَليبِ في كُلِّ مَرَّةٍ كُنْتُ أَزورُها مَعَ أَبي أَوْ مَعَ أُمّي، أَوْ في كُلِّ مَرَّةٍ كُنّا نَزورُها أَنا وَأَبي وَأُمّي. وَكُنّا نَأْكُلُ عِنْدَها الحَلَوِياتِ مِثْلَ الأَرُزِّ بِالحَليبِ وَالمُهَلَّبِيَّةِ وَالمَعْمولِ وَلَيالي لُبْنان وَالبَقْلاوَة.

She said, 'But these are Atra shoes.'"

Maya understood the phrase and laughed. "How funny Souad is!" Maya said happily.

"What does it mean, Maya?" her brother asked.

"The woman means 'autre chose' in French. [1]

Adel laughed too, then said, "A funny seamstress."

Then Maya said, "These people, like Auntie Souad and Mrs. Zeina, are smart."

"Yes, my sweetheart, Souad was an intelligent lady, and she used to love smart people, too. And her taste in sewing was beautiful. Everyone loved her taste. She learned sewing at a young age in one of the old neighborhoods of Beirut, and she had clients in Beirut and other cities. She had clients in the villages, too.

She would offer me chocolate with milk or cocoa with milk every time I visited her with my father or mother or whenever I visited her with both my father and mother. And we also used to eat sweets, such as roz bihalib (rice pudding), mouhallabiah (pudding), maamoul, Layali Lubnan (Lebanse nights), and baklava.

---

[1] The pun means the following: Souad was a funny lady, so she pronounced the expression "autre chose" as "atra shoes" just to make Samir laugh because he showed discontent with having more trousers (a polite way to say no to the trousers because of their color). In Lebanon, the expression "autro chose" has been borrowed from the French language to mean "really original or nothing compares to it." Souad wanted to say that the trousers would look great and that no... (continued on page 29)

في ذلِكَ اليَوْمِ هِيَ قالَتْ: 'سَنَتَناوَلُ الغَداءَ بَعْدَ قَليلٍ يا سَميرُ. ثُمَّ أَنْتَ تَشْرَبُ الكاكاوَ بِالحَليبِ وَتَأْكُلُ البَقْلاوَةَ. وَنَحْنُ، أَنا وَأَبوكَ وَزَوْجي، سَنَشْرَبُ القَهْوَةَ فَقَطْ. البَقْلاوَةُ لِناسٍ في عُمَرِنا يا ابْنَ ابْنِ خالي مِثْلُ هَذِهِ السِّكّينِ. سَوْفَ تَفْهَمُ المَعْنى يَوْمًا مِنَ الأَيّامِ' وَحَمَلَتْ سِكّينًا كانَتْ عَلى عُلْبَةِ الحَلْوى، وَقالَتْ: 'اُنْظُرْ يا سَميرُ، مِنْ هُنا يايْ، لَكِنْ مِنْ هُنا آيْ.'" [1]

ضَحِكَ عادِلٌ ومايا كَثيرًا كَثيرًا. مَرَّةً هُوَ يَقولُ "يايْ" وَأُخْتُهُ تَقولُ "آيْ"، وَمَرَّةً أُخْتُهُ تَقولُ "يايْ" وَهُوَ يَقولُ "آيْ".

نادى عادِلٌ أُمَّهُ: "ماما ... ماما ... نُريدُ الكاكاوَ بِالحَليبِ. حَضِّري لَنا، مِنْ فَضْلِكِ. لَنا وَلِجَدّي سَميرٍ أَيْضًا."

اِبْتَسَمَ الجَدُّ وَقالَ: "في عُمْري، السُّكَّرُ ..."

"آيْ، آيْ" ضَحِكَ مَرَّةً أُخْرى، وَضَحِكَ سَميرٌ كَثيرًا، وَضَحِكَتْ أُمُّ عادِلٍ في المَطْبَخِ بِصَوْتٍ مُرْتَفِعٍ. أَحَبَّ الوَلَدانِ العِبارَتَيْنِ.

بَعْدَ قَليلٍ، سَأَلَتْ مايا: "لِماذا عِنْدَ سُعادَ بَقْلاوَةٌ؟ هَلْ هِيَ وَزَوْجُها يَأْكُلانِ الحَلَوِياتِ؟"

On that day, she said, 'We will have lunch shortly, Samir. Then you'll drink cocoa with milk and eat baklava. And we—your father, my husband, and I—are just going to drink coffee. Baklava, for people our age, is similar to this knife. You will understand the meaning one day. And she took a knife off the candy box, and said, 'Look, Samir, from here "yay," but from here "ay".'"[1]

Adel and Maya laughed a lot. One time he says "yay," and his sister says "ay," and another time, his sister says "yay," and he says "ay."

Adel called his mother, "Mom... Mom! We want cocoa with milk. Make us some, please. For us and Grandpa Samir, too."

The grandfather smiled and said, "At my age, sugar..."

"Ay, ay," they laughed again, Samir laughed a lot, and Adel's mother laughed out loud in the kitchen. The children loved the two expressions.

After a while, Maya asked, "Why does Souad have baklava? Do she and her husband eat sweets?"

---

[1] ياي ("yay") is a word used to express admiration, similar to 'wow' in English. آيْ ("ay") is the sound someone makes when in pain.

(continued from page 27) ... other trousers would compare. "Atra shoes" combines two words: the first is Arabic and means "the softest," while the second is English. The whole expression, then, would mean "the softest shoes," and all people would choose soft and comfortable shoes suitable for walking long distances in opposition to hard, uncomfortable shoes. It is very common for the Lebanese to adopt French words in their everyday talks due to the French influence in the Middle East post the First World War.

"لا يا حَبيبَتي. الحَلَوِياتُ لِلزَّبوناتِ والجاراتِ وَلَنا فَقَط. في رَأيِكِ يا مايا، أما كانَتْ سُعادُ تُحِبُّ النّاسَ؟"

"أَظُنُّ بَلى."

"نَعَمْ، كانَتْ كَريمَةً، رَحِمَها اللهُ. وَكانَتْ تُحِبُّ كُلَّ النّاسِ. كُلُّ النّاسِ والزَّبوناتِ والجاراتِ يُحِبّونَها وَيَشْرَبونَ القَهْوَةَ مَعَها. كُلُّهُمْ يَأْكُلونَ عِنْدَها الحَلَوِياتِ العَرَبِيَّةَ."

أَكْمَلَ سَميرٌ قِصَّتَهُ: "بَعْدَ ذَلِكَ، رَجَعنا إلى البَيْتِ. أَبي قال كُلَّ الوَقْتِ: 'هَذا اللَّوْنُ جَميلٌ، والقُماشُ مِنْ مَحَلٍّ مُمْتازٍ في شارِعٍ بَيْروتيٍّ كُلُّهُ مَحَلّاتٌ جَميلَةٌ. سَتَرى. سَيُحِبُّ كُلُّ التَّلاميذِ والمُعَلِّماتِ بِنْطالَكَ. سَتَلْبَسُهُ، وَسَيَقولونَ إنَّهُ أَنيقٌ.'"

"هَلْ كانَتْ أُمُّكَ تَعْمَلُ يا جَدّي؟" أَرادَ عادِلٌ أَنْ يَعْرِفَ وَهوَ يَنْظُرُ لِوَقْتٍ طَويلٍ إلى لَوْحَةٍ عَلى جِدارِ البَهْوِ. في اللَّوْحَةِ امْرَأَةٌ وابْنَتُها الصَّغيرَةُ داخِلَ حَديقَةٍ مِنَ الوَرْدِ الأَحْمَرِ."

"لا يا صَغيري. أُمّي، رَحِمَها اللهُ، كانَتْ رَبَّةَ بَيْتٍ. كانَتْ تَعْتَني بِأُسْرَتِها: تَطْبُخُ، وَتَغْسِلُ الثِّيابَ، وَتُدَرِّسُني الإمْلاءَ والْجُغْرافيا وَ ..."

"No, my love. Sweets are only for customers, neighbors, and us. Maya, in your opinion, didn't Souad love people?"

"I think so."

"Yes, she was generous; may God have mercy on her. And she loved all people. Everyone, including customers and neighbors, used to love her and drink coffee with her. They would all eat Arabic sweets at her home."

Samir continued his story. "After that, we went home. My father said all the time: 'This color is beautiful, and the cloth is from an excellent store on a Beiruti street full of beautiful stores. You will see. All the students and teachers will love your trousers. You will wear them, and everyone will say that they are elegant.'"

"Did your mother use to work, Grandpa?" Adel wanted to know while staring at a painting on the parlor's wall. In the painting, a woman and her young daughter are in a garden of red roses.

"No, my little one. My mother, may God have mercy on her, was a housewife. She would take care of her family. She cooked, washed clothes, and taught me dictation, geography, and…"

ثُمَّ سَأَلَ عادِلٌ مَرَّةً أُخرى: "لِماذا لا تَروي لَنا قِصَصًا أُخرى عَنْ تِلْكَ الأَيّامِ؟"

"أَروي لَكُما وَلكِنْ هذِهِ اللَّيْلَةَ لا. هذِهِ اللَّيْلَةَ أَروي قِصَّتي عَنِ المَدْرَسَةِ. ثُمَّ نَتَناوَلُ العَشاءَ وَنُشاهِدُ التِّلْفازَ قَليلًا. بَعْدَ ذلِكَ نَنامُ. غَدًا سَتَسْتَيْقِظانِ باكِرًا، أَلَيْسَ كَذلِكَ؟"

"بَلى، هذا صَحيحٌ."

بَعْدَ قَليلٍ، أَتَتْ أُمُّ عادِلٍ مِنَ المَطْبَخِ وَمَعَها ثَلاثَةُ أَكْوابٍ مِنَ الكاكاوِ بِالحَليبِ. قَدَّمَتْ كوبًا لِكُلِّ واحِدٍ، ثُمَّ قَدَّمَتْ صَحْنًا فيهِ البَسْكَويتُ. قالَتْ: "بِالهَناءِ والشِّفاءِ."

"شُكْرًا يا أُمّي."

"شُكْرًا يا أُمَّ عادِلٍ."

"أَهْلًا وَسَهْلًا بِكَ يا عَمّي."

"وَالآنَ، نُريدُ أَنْ نَسْتَمِعَ إِلى القِصَّةِ كُلِّها. ماذا بَعْدُ؟"

"أَتى يَوْمُ الاِثْنَيْنِ يا مايا، وَأَتى المَوْعِدُ مَعَ سُعادَ. قالَ أَبي بَعْدَ الغَداءِ: 'سَأَذْهَبُ إِلى اِبْنَةِ عَمَّتي لِأَشْرَبَ القَهْوَةَ مَعَها وَمَعَ زَوْجِها. سَأَرْجِعُ بَعْدَ ساعَتَيْنِ وَمَعي البِنْطالُ.'

Then Adel asked again, "Why don't you tell us other stories about those days?"

"I will, but not tonight. Tonight, I will just tell my story about school. Then, we will have dinner and watch some TV. After that, we will go to sleep. Tomorrow you will get up early, won't you?"

"Yes, that is true."

Soon, Umm Adel came from the kitchen with three cups of cocoa with milk. She served a cup to each, then a plate with cookies. "Bon appetit," she said.

"Thank you, Mom."

"Thank you, Umm Adel."

"You're welcome, Father-in-law."

"Now, we want to hear the whole story. What happened next?"

"It was Monday, the day to go to Souad. After lunch, my father said, 'I will go to my cousin to have coffee with her and her husband. I'll be back with the trousers in two hours.'

رَجَعَ أَبِي وَمَعَهُ كِيسٌ أَبْيَضُ. قَالَ لِأُمِّي: 'تَفَضَّلِي يا أُمَّ سَمِيرٍ. إِنَّهُ في الكِيسِ.'"

لَكِنِ الجَدُّ قَالَ: "هَيّا بِنا نَشْرَبُ الكَاكاوَ بِالحَلِيبِ ثُمَّ نُتابِعُ."

في هَذا الوَقْتِ، أَخْبَرَ الوَلَدانِ جَدَّهُما عَنْ أَلْعابِ الكُمْبيوتِرِ وَأَلْعابِ الموبايلِ والعُطْلَةِ الصَّيْفِيَّةِ.

عادِلٌ كانَ يُحِبُّ أَنْ يَرْسَمَ، فَقالَ لِسَمِيرٍ إِنَّهُ رَسَمَ لَوْحَةً كَبِيرَةً. وَقالَ لَهُ إِنَّ والِدَهُ سَيُعَلِّقُها عَلى جِدارِ غُرْفَةِ الجُلوسِ.

وَمايا تَذْهَبُ إِلى مَدْرَسَةٍ لِلرَّقْصِ في مَساءِ يَوْمِ الثُّلاثاءِ، فَرَقَصَتْ قَلِيلًا أَمامَ جَدِّها.

قالَ سَمِيرٌ: "ما شاءَ اللّٰهُ يا حَفِيدَتي وَيا حَفِيدي. هَذا رَقْصٌ جَمِيلٌ وَهَذِهِ لَوْحَةٌ جَمِيلَةٌ. أَنا سَعِيدٌ بِكُما."

"أَكْمِلِ القِصَّةَ يا جَدّي."

أَكْمَلَ سَمِيرٌ: "عادَ أَبي وَبِيَدِهِ الكِيسُ. وَضَعَهُ عَلى الصّوفا. خَرَجَتْ أُمِّي مِنَ البَهْوِ وَسارَتْ إِلى الصّوفا في غُرْفَةِ الجُلوسِ. أَخْرَجَتِ البِنْطالَ مِنَ الكِيسِ، وَقالَتْ: 'البِنْطالُ رائِعٌ! أَنا أَعْرِفُ أَنَّ ذَوْقَ سُعادَ جَمِيلٌ.'

My father came back with a white bag. He said to my mother, 'Here you go, Umm Samir... They're in the bag.'"

But the grandfather said, "Let's drink our cocoa with milk and then continue the story."

Then, the children told their grandfather about computer games, mobile games, and the summer holidays.

Adel liked to draw, so he told Samir that he had painted a big picture. He told him that his father would hang it on the living room wall.

And Maya goes to a dance school every Tuesday evening, and she danced in front of her grandfather.

Samir said, "How nice, my granddaughter and my grandson. This is a beautiful dance, and this is a beautiful painting. I am glad."

"Continue with the story, Grandpa."

Samir continued. "My father returned with the bag in his hand. He put it on the couch. My mother came out of the parlor and walked over to the couch in the living room. She took the trousers out of the bag and said, 'The trousers are great! I knew that Souad had good taste.'

نَظَرْتُ إِلى البِنْطالِ وَقُلْتُ: 'ماما ... في الحَقيقَةِ، لا أُحِبُّ لَوْنَهُ. هذا اللَّوْنُ لِلْكِبارِ في السِّنِّ.'

أَجابَتْ: 'لَوْنُهُ جَميلٌ جِدًّا في فَصْلِ الشِّتاءِ يا صَغيري. لَيْسَ لَوْنًا لِلْكِبارِ في السِّنِّ. لَيْسَ هُناكَ لَوْنٌ لِلْكِبارِ وَلَوْنٌ لِلصِّغارِ. هَيّا! اُدْخُلْ إِلى غُرْفَتِكَ والبَسْهُ.'

دَخَلْتُ وَما خَرَجْتُ. نادَتْني: 'أَيْنَ أَنْتَ؟ اُخْرُجْ لِأَراهُ عَلَيْكَ!'

فَتَحْتُ بابَ الغُرْفَةِ وَقُلْتُ: 'البِنْطالُ لَيْسَ مَقاسي. خَلَعْتُهُ وَوَضَعْتُهُ عَلى السَّريرِ.'

قالَتْ أُمّي: 'هَلْ هَذِهِ نُكْتَةٌ؟ هذا لَيْسَ صَحيحًا! سُعادُ مِنَ الخَيّاطاتِ المُمْتازاتِ في بَيْروتَ.'

قُلْتُ: 'سُعادُ كانَتْ خَيّاطَةً مُمْتازَةً. لَكِنِ الآنَ هِيَ سَيِّدَةٌ كَبيرَةٌ في السِّنِّ. لا شَكَّ في أَنَّها أَصْبَحَتْ لا تَرى جَيِّدًا. يَداها تَرْجُفانِ، والبِنْطالُ قَصيرٌ، وَسَوْفَ يَظُنُّ النّاسُ أَنَّهُ لَيْسَ لي.'

لَكِنْ أُمّي أَجابَتْ: 'هَيّا! اِلْبَسْهُ مَرَّةً أُخْرى يا ابني. أُريدُ أَنْ أَراهُ عَلَيْكَ. آهِ، والْبَسْ مَعَهُ كَنْزَةَ الصّوفِ ... الكَنْزَةَ الخَضْراءَ الجَديدَةَ.'"

I looked at the trousers and said, 'Mom... I really don't like this color. This color is for old people.'

She replied, 'It is a very beautiful color in winter, my child. It is not a color for the old. There isn't a color for the old and another for the young. Come on, go to your room and put them on.'

I went into my bedroom and didn't come out. She called me, 'Where are you? Come out so I can see them on you!'

I opened my bedroom door and said, 'The trousers are not my size. I took them off and put them on the bed.'

My mom said: 'Is this a joke? That's not true! Souad is one of the best seamstresses in Beirut.'

I said, 'Souad used to be an excellent seamstress, but now she is an old lady. There is no doubt that she no longer sees well. Her hands shake, the trousers are short, and people will think they're not mine.'

But my mother replied, 'Come on, put them on again, my son. I want to see them on you. Oh, and put on the wool sweater—the new green one.'"

سَأَلَ عادِلٌ الرَّجُلَ الجالِسَ بَيْنَهُ وَبَيْنَ أُخْتِهِ: "يا جَدّي، لِماذا كانَتْ أُمُّكَ هَكَذا؟ أنا وَمايا نَقولُ لِأُمِّنا: لا. وَهِيَ تُجيبُ: لا مُشْكِلَةَ. كَما تُريدانِ."

"يا حَبيبي، كانَتْ أُمّي تَخافُ عَلَيَّ مِنَ البَرْدِ في المَدْرَسَةِ. كانَتْ تُحِبُّني كَثيرًا، وَلا تُريدُني أَنْ أَمْرَضَ."

"وَماذا فَعَلْتَ في الأَخيرِ يا جَدّي؟"

"في الأَخيرِ، قالَتْ أُمّي: اُنْظُرْ كَمْ هُوَ جَميلٌ عَلَيْكَ مَعَ هَذِهِ الكَنْزَةِ الخَضْراءِ! هَذا هُوَ مَقاسُكَ. سَلِمَتْ يَداكِ يا سُعادُ وَأَطالَ اللَّهُ عُمرَكِ. سَتَلْبَسُهُما غَدًا، أَلَيْسَ كَذَلِكَ؟"

"مِسْكينٌ أَنْتَ يا جَدّي. في الماضي كانَتِ الأُمُّ قاسِيَةً. لا أُحِبُّ هَذا."

"قاسِيَةٌ قَليلًا، وَلَكِنِ الأُمُّ دائِمًا تُريدُ الشَّيْءَ الجَميلَ لِأَبْنائِها."

"لا يا جَدّي! أُمُّكَ كانَتْ قاسِيَةً كَثيرًا. أُمُّنا لا تَسْتَخْدِمُ مَعَنا أَفْعالَ الأَمْرِ."

نادَتْ أُمُّ عادِلٍ ابْنَها: "يا عادِلُ! يا عادِلُ! تَفَضَّلْ إلى المَطْبَخِ الآنَ وَبِسُرْعَةٍ. ساعِدْني لِنَأْخُذَ الصُّحونَ إلى مائِدَةِ غُرْفَةِ الطَّعامِ."

Adel asked the man sitting between him and his sister, "Grandpa, why was your mother like this? Maya and I say 'no' to our mother. And she answers: 'No problem. As you wish'."

"My love, my mother was worried that I would feel cold at school. She loved me so much and didn't want me to get sick."

"And what did you do in the end, Grandpa?"

"Finally, my mother said, 'Look how beautiful you look in that green sweater! This is your size. Thank you, Souad, and may God prolong your life. You will wear them tomorrow, won't you?"

"Poor you, grandfather. In the past, mothers were harsh. I don't like this."

A little harsh, but a mother always wants something nice for her children.

"No, grandpa! Your mother was very harsh. Our mother does not use imperative verbs with us."

Umm Adel called out to her son, "Adel! Oh, Adel! Come to the kitchen right away. Help me take the plates to the dining-room table."

ضَحِكَ الثَّلاثَةُ وَأَصْبَحَ وَجْهُ عادِلٍ أَحْمَرَ.

عانَقَ سَميرٌ حَفيدَيْهِ وَأَنْهى قِصَّتَهُ:

"وَأَتى الغَدُ. طَقْسٌ بارِدٌ وَريحٌ شَديدَةٌ. تَناوَلْتُ الفَطورَ بَعْدَ أَنْ غَسَلْتُ وَجْهي. ثُمَّ نَظَّفْتُ أَسْناني بِالفُرْشاةِ وَالمَعْجونِ. وَفي غُرْفَةِ النَّوْمِ، لَبِسْتُ ذَلِكَ البِنْطالَ البُنِّيَّ وَمَعَهُ لَبِسْتُ الكَنْزَةَ الخَضْراءَ. وَتَحْتَ تِلْكَ الكَنْزَةِ، لَبِسْتُ واحِدَةً أُخْرى.

أَرادَتْ أُمّي أَنْ تَرْويَ لي قِصَصًا مُضْحِكَةً، لَكِنّي ما كُنْتُ سَعيدًا لا في البَيْتِ وَقْتَ الفَطورِ وَلا في الشّارِعِ وَنَحْنُ نَنْتَظِرُ باصَ المَدْرَسَةِ. وَصَلَ الباصُ وَقُلْتُ لَها: مَعَ السَّلامَةِ.

بَعْدَ تَحِيَّةِ الصَّباحِ لِلسّائِقِ، ذَهَبْتُ إِلى مَقْعَدٍ بَعيدٍ عَنْ كُلِّ التَّلاميذِ. خَلَعْتُ مِعْطَفي وَقُبَّعَتي وَنَظَرْتُ إِلى بِنْطالي. كانَ حُزْني كَبيرًا. وَصَلْنا إِلى المَدْرَسَةِ وَأَنا ذَهَبْتُ مِنَ المَلْعَبِ إِلى صَفّي. ما تَكَلَّمْتُ مَعَ زُمَلائي.

The three laughed, and Adel's face turned red.

Samir hugged his grandchildren and finished his story:

"The next day came. The weather was cold and windy. I had breakfast after I had washed my face. Then I brushed my teeth with a toothbrush and toothpaste. And in the bedroom, I put on those brown trousers and wore the green sweater. And under that sweater, I put on another one.

My mother wanted to tell me funny stories, but I was not happy, neither at home at breakfast time nor on the street while we were waiting for the school bus. The bus arrived, and I said 'bye' to her.

After saying good morning to the driver, I went to a seat far away from all the students. I took off my coat and hat and looked at my trousers. My grief was great. We got to school, and I went straight from the playground to my class. I didn't talk to my classmates.

في الصَّفِّ جَلَسْتُ عَلى مَقْعَدي، في مَكاني، كُلَّ الوَقْتِ. وَفي دَرْسِ الإِمْلاءِ الْعَرَبِيِّ طَلَبَتْ مِنّي المُعَلِّمَةُ أَنْ أَذْهَبَ إِلى السَّبّورَةِ بَعْدَ أَمينٍ. كُنْتُ أَعْرِفُ كَيْفَ نَكْتُبُ الكَلِمَتَيْنِ. كُلُّ الكَلِماتِ سَهْلَةٌ. لَكِنّي قُلْتُ لِلمُعَلِّمَةِ: 'لا أُريدُ أَنْ أَذْهَبَ إِلى السَّبّورَةِ!' شَعَرْتُ بِخَجَلٍ كَبيرٍ أَمامَ التَّلاميذِ مِنْ ذَلِكَ البِنْطالِ. وَعِنْدَما سَأَلَتْني المُعَلِّمَةُ أَكْثَرَ مِنْ مَرَّةٍ لِماذا لا أُريدُ أَنْ أَكْتُبَ، خَرَجَتْ دُموعٌ كَثيرَةٌ مِنْ عَيْنَيَّ!"

In class, I took my seat and remained there throughout the entire school day. In the Arabic dictation lesson, the teacher asked me to go to the blackboard after Amin. I knew how the two words were spelled. All the words were easy. But I told the teacher I didn't want to go to the blackboard. I felt very embarrassed in front of the students about those trousers. And when the teacher asked me more than once why I did not want to write, many tears came out of my eyes!"

أَسْئِلَةُ الفَهْمِ

1. في أَيِّ صَفٍّ كانَ سَميرٌ؟
2. في أَيَّةِ مَدْرَسَةٍ دَرَسَ سَميرٌ؟
3. كَيْفَ كانَ الجَوُّ في ذَلِكَ اليَوْمِ مِنْ أَيَّامِ شَهْرِ يَنايَرَ؟
4. هَلْ كانَ سَميرٌ سَعيدًا في ذَلِكَ اليَوْمِ؟
5. أَيْنَ يَنْتَظِرُ سَميرٌ الباصَ كُلَّ يَوْمٍ؟
6. هَلْ كانَ سَميرٌ وَحْدَهُ في الشّارِعِ يَنْتَظِرُ باصَ المَدْرَسَةِ في ذَلِكَ اليَوْمِ؟
7. لِماذا لَبِسَ سَميرٌ مِعْطَفًا وَوَضَعَ قُبَّعَةً؟
8. أَيْنَ جَلَسَ سَميرٌ في الباصِ؟
9. لِماذا كانَ سَميرٌ مِثْلَ شَجَرَةٍ؟
10. أَيْنَ كانَ يَجْلِسُ سَميرٌ وَحَفيداهُ؟
11. كَمْ عُمْرُ الوَلَدَيْنِ؟
12. كَيْفَ يَصِفُ سَميرٌ التِّلْميذَ أَمينًا؟

Comprehension Questions

1. What grade was Samir in at school?
2. Where did Samir go to school?
3. What was the weather like on that January day?
4. Was Samir happy that day?
5. Where does Samir wait for the bus every day?
6. Was Samir alone on the street waiting for the school bus that day?
7. Why did Samir wear a coat and a hat?
8. Where did Samir sit on the bus?
9. Why did Samir look like a tree?
10. Where were Samir and his two grandchildren sitting?
11. How old are the two children?
12. How does Samir describe the student Amin?

13. كَيْفَ يَصِفُ سَميرٌ مُعَلِّمَةَ اللُّغَةِ العَرَبِيَّةِ؟

14. هَلْ تُحِبُّ مايا مُعَلِّمَةَ اللُّغَةِ العَرَبِيَّةِ في مَدْرَسَتِها؟

15. كَيْفَ ساعَدَتِ المُعَلِّمَةُ أمينًا في الأخيرِ؟

16. لِماذا عادَ أمينٌ إلى مَقْعَدِهِ وَهُوَ يَبْكي؟

17. ماذا تَعْمَلُ سُعادُ؟

18. ماذا كانَ عَلى الطّاوِلَةِ الصَّغيرَةِ بِالقُرْبِ مِنْ سَريرِ زَوْجِ سُعادَ؟

19. هَلْ أُمُّ سَميرٍ اِشْتَرَتْ قِطْعَةَ القُماشِ؟

20. ماذا تُريدُ أُمُّ سَميرٍ مِنْ سُعادَ؟

21. ماذا قالَ أبو سَميرٍ عَنْ فِكْرَةِ زَوْجَتِهِ؟

22. لِماذا كانَتْ سُعادُ في حاجَةٍ إلى الكَثيرِ مِنَ المالِ؟

23. في أَيِّ يَوْمٍ ذَهَبَ سَميرٌ وَأبوهُ إلى الخَيّاطَةِ؟

24. في أَيِّ يَوْمٍ كانَ البِنْطالُ جاهِزًا؟

13. How would he describe the Arabic language teacher?
14. Does Maya like the Arabic language teacher in her school?
15. How did the teacher help Amin?
16. Why did Amin return to his seat crying?
17. What does Souad do?
18. What was on the little table near the bed of Souad's husband?
19. Did Samir's mother buy the piece of cloth?
20. What does Samir's mother want to do with the piece of cloth?
21. What does Samir's father say about his wife's idea?
22. Why did Souad need so much money?
23. On what day did Samir and his father go to the seamstress?
24. What day were the trousers ready?

25. كَيْفَ تَعْرِفُ مايا أَنَّ سُعادَ امْرَأَةٌ ذَكِيَّةٌ؟

26. مِنْ أَيْنَ زَبوناتُ سُعادَ؟

27. أَيَّةَ حَلَوْياتٍ تُحَضِّرُ سُعادُ؟

28. هَلْ كانَتْ أُمُّ سَميرٍ تَعْمَلُ؟

29. ماذا رَسَمَ عادِلٌ؟

30. إِلى أَيْنَ كانَتْ مايا تَذْهَبُ كُلَّ يَوْمِ ثُلاثاءٍ؟

31. لِماذا لا يُحِبُّ سَميرٌ البِنْطالَ؟

32. هَلْ قالَ سَميرٌ إِنَّ سُعادَ خَيّاطَةٌ مُمْتازَةٌ؟

33. لِماذا يَقولُ سَميرٌ إِنَّ أُمَّهُ كانَتْ قاسِيَةً قَليلًا وَلَيْسَ كَثيرًا؟

34. لِماذا ضَحِكَ الثَّلاثَةُ وَأَصْبَحَ وَجْهُ عادِلٍ أَحْمَرَ قَبْلَ نِهايَةِ القِصَّةِ؟

35. ماذا لَبِسَ سَميرٌ تَحْتَ كَنْزَةِ الصّوفِ الخَضْراءِ؟

25. How does Maya know that Souad is an intelligent woman?
26. Where are Souad's customers from?
27. What kind of sweets does Souad prepare?
28. Did Samir's mother have a job?
29. What did Adel draw?
30. Where did Maya go every Tuesday?
31. Why doesn't Samir like the trousers?
32. Did Samir say that Souad is an excellent seamstress?
33. Why does Samir say that his mother was a little harsh and not very harsh?
34. Why did the three laugh, and Adel's face turn red before the end of the story?
35. What did Samir wear under the green wool sweater?

أَسْئِلَةٌ لِلْمُناقَشَةِ

1. هَلْ جَيِّدٌ أَنْ تَقولَ أُمُّ سَميرٍ لِابْنِها ماذا يَلْبَسُ؟ هَلْ أُمُّكَ هَكَذا أَوْ كانَتْ هَكَذا؟

2. لِماذا يَرْوي سَميرٌ قِصَّتَهُ لِحَفيدَيْهِ؟

3. هَلْ كانَ عِنْدَكَ مُعَلِّمَةٌ تَشْرَحُ الدُّروسَ جَيِّدًا وَتَقولُ النُّكَتَ؟ مَنْ هِيَ؟ كَيْفَ كانَتْ؟

4. هَلْ، في رَأْيِكَ، أُمُّ سَميرٍ أُمٌّ ذَكِيَّةٌ؟ لِمَ نَعَمْ أَوْ لِمَ لا؟

5. في مُجْتَمَعِكَ، هَلْ تَزورُ المَرْأَةُ جارَتَها لِتَشْرَبَ القَهْوَةَ وَتَأْكُلَ الحَلَوِيّاتِ عِنْدَها مِثْلَ جاراتِ الخَيّاطَةِ سُعادَ؟

6. هَلْ سُعادُ امْرَأَةٌ حَزينَةٌ أَمِ امْرَأَةٌ سَعيدَةٌ؟ كَيْفَ تَعْرِفُ؟

7. أُمُّ سَميرٍ وَأَبوهُ ساعَدا سُعادَ وَزَوْجَها. هَلْ أَنْتَ تُساعِدُ رَجُلًا أَوِ امْرَأَةً في حاجَةٍ إلى مالٍ؟ كَيْفَ؟

8. هَلْ شَعَرْتَ بِالْخَجَلِ الكَبيرِ أَمامَ النّاسِ في يَوْمٍ مِنَ الأَيّامِ وَأَنْتَ صَغيرٌ في السِّنِّ؟ ماذا حَدَثَ مَعَكَ؟

Discussion Questions

1. Is it good for Samir's mother to tell her son what to wear? Is/Was your mother like this?
2. Why does Samir tell his story to his two grandchildren?
3. Did you have a teacher who explained lessons well and told jokes? Who was she? How and what did she look like?
4. Do you think Umm Samir is an intelligent mother? Why or why not?
5. In your society, does a woman visit her neighbor to drink coffee and eat sweets with her like the seamstress Souad's neighbors do?
6. Is Souad a sad or a happy woman? How would you know?
7. Samir's mother and father helped Souad and her husband. Would you help a man or a woman in need financially? How would you do that?
8. Did you ever feel very shy in front of people when you were young? What happened with you?

9. في رَأيِكَ، لِماذا أُمُّ عادِلٍ ما نادَتْ مايا لِتُساعِدَها في أَنْ تَأْخُذَ الصُّحونَ مِنَ المَطبَخِ؟

10. أَيَّةَ شَخْصِيَّةٍ في القِصَّةِ أَحْبَبْتَ كَثيرًا؟ لِماذا؟

11. ماذا تَعْرِفُ الآنَ عَنِ المُجْتَمَعِ اللُّبنانيِّ مِنْ خِلالِ هَذِهِ القِصَّةِ؟

12. اُكْتُبْ حِوارًا قَصيرًا فيهِ يَتَكَلَّمُ سَميرٌ وَزَوْجُ سُعادَ بَعْدَ الغَداءِ.

9. In your opinion, why did Adel's mother not call Maya to help her take the dishes from the kitchen?

10. Which character in the story did you like the most? Why?

11. What do you now know about Lebanese society in light of this story?

12. Write a short dialogue in which Samir and Souad's husband are talking after lunch.

صَحيحٌ أَمْ خَطَأٌ أَمْ لا نَعْرِفُ؟
صَحِّحِ الجُمْلَةَ الخَطَأ.

1. ____ كانَتْ مَدْرَسَةُ سَميرٍ قَريبَةً مِنْ مَدينَةِ بَيْروتَ.
2. ____ كُلَّ يَوْمٍ يَنْتَظِرُ سَميرٌ باصَ المَدْرَسَةِ مَعَ أُمِّهِ.
3. ____ أُمُّ سَميرٍ تَروي لِابْنِها قِصَصًا مُضْحِكَةً لِأَنَّهُ كانَ حَزينًا.
4. ____ في الباصِ جَلَسَ سَميرٌ بِجانِبِ تِلْميذٍ آخَرَ.
5. ____ المُعَلِّمَةُ طَلَبَتْ مِنْ أمينٍ أَنْ يَكْتُبَ أَرْبَعَ كَلِماتٍ عَلى السَّبّورَةِ.
6. ____ أمينٌ خَطُّهُ جَميلٌ وَبِنْطالُهُ نَظيفٌ.
7. ____ مُعَلِّمَةُ اللُّغَةِ العَرَبِيَّةِ في مَدْرَسَةِ سَميرٍ كانَتْ تَغْضَبُ عَلى التِّلْميذِ الكَسولِ.
8. ____ مايا تُحِبُّ مُعَلِّمَةَ اللُّغَةِ العَرَبِيَّةِ في مَدْرَسَتِها.
9. ____ كَتَبَ أمينٌ الكَلِماتِ كُلَّها خَطَأً.

True, False, or Unknown?
Correct the wrong sentence.

1. _____ Samir's school was close to the city of Beirut.

2. _____ Every day, Samir would wait for the school bus with his mother.

3. _____ Samir's mother would tell her son funny stories because he was sad.

4. _____ On the bus, Samir sat next to another student.

5. _____ The teacher asked Amin to write four words on the board.

6. _____ Amin has beautiful handwriting, and his trousers are clean.

7. _____ The Arabic language teacher at Samir's school used to get angry at the lazy student.

8. _____ Maya loves the Arabic teacher at her school.

9. _____ Amin spelled all the words wrong.

10. ___ في الصَّفِّ أمينٌ يَجْلِسُ عَلى مَقْعَدٍ أمامَ مَقْعَدِ سَميرٍ.

11. ___ في الماضي، كانَ زَوْجُ سُعادَ يَعْمَلُ في بَنْكٍ.

12. ___ أبو سَميرٍ اِشْتَرى لِزَوْجَتِهِ قِطْعَةَ قُماشٍ لَونُها أزْرَقُ.

13. ___ سُعادُ خالَةُ سَميرٍ وَهِيَ تَسكُنُ في بَيْروتَ.

14. ___ أُمُّ عادِلٍ كانَتْ تَطْبُخُ الدَّجاجَ بِالأَرُزِّ تِلْكَ اللَّيْلَةَ.

15. ___ أبو سَميرٍ كانَ عِنْدَهُ سَيّارَةٌ كَبيرَةٌ لَوْنُها أحْمَرُ.

16. ___ سُعادُ تَعَلَّمَتِ الخِياطَةَ في بَيْروتَ في عُمْرٍ صَغيرٍ.

17. ___ كانَ سَميرٌ يَزورُ سُعادَ مَعَ أبيهِ لِأنَّ أُمَّهُ لا تُحِبُّ سُعادَ كَثيرًا.

18. ___ كانَتْ أُمُّ سَميرٍ تُدَرِّسُ اِبْنَها الجُغْرافيا والإمْلاءَ.

10. _____ In the classroom, Amin sits on a bench in front of Samir's bench.
11. _____ In the past, Souad's husband worked in a bank.
12. _____ Abu Samir bought his wife a piece of blue cloth.
13. _____ Souad is Samir's maternal aunt, and she lives in Beirut.
14. _____ Adel's mother was cooking chicken with rice that night.
15. _____ Abu Samir had a big red car.
16. _____ Suad learned sewing in Beirut at a young age.
17. _____ Samir used to visit Souad with his father because his mother did not like Souad very much.
18. _____ Umm Samir used to teach her son geography and dictation.

19. ____ يَطْلُبُ عادِلٌ مِنْ جَدِّهِ قِصَصًا عَنْ حَياتِهِ في الماضي.

20. ____ سَميرٌ هُوَ والِدُ أَمْ عادِلٍ.

19. _____ Adel asks his grandfather for stories about his life in the past.

20. _____ Samir is the father of Umm Adel.

اِملَأ الفَراغَ بِالفِعْلِ المُناسِبِ.

1. _____ سَميرٌ لِحَفيدَيهِ قِصَّةً عَنْ أَيّامِ المَدرَسَةِ.
   أ. يَزورُ   ب. يَروي   ج. يَقْرَأُ

2. ذَلِكَ اليَومُ _____ يَومًا مُمْطِرًا وَحَزينًا.
   أ. كانَ   ب. سَيَكونُ   ج. يَكونُ

3. _____ الهَواءُ الغُيومَ إلى فَوقُ.
   أ. يَرفَعُ   ب. يَرمي   ج. يَذهَبُ

4. _____ أُمُّ سَميرٍ أَنْ تَروِيَ قِصَصًا مُضْحِكَةً لِابْنِها.
   أ. سَمِعَتْ   ب. حاوَلَتْ   ج. قالَتْ

5. سَميرٌ _____ مِعْطَفَهُ وَقُبَّعَتَهُ في الباصِ.
   أ. حَمَلَ   ب. أَخَذَ   ج. خَلَعَ

6. الوَلَدانِ _____ عَلى الأَريكَةِ في البَهوِ.
   أ. يَنامانِ   ب. يَسْتَلْقِيانِ   ج. يَجْلِسانِ

7. التَّلاميذُ _____ مِنْ مُعَلِّمَةِ اللُّغَةِ العَرَبِيَّةِ.
   أ. يُحِبّونَ   ب. يَخافُ   ج. يَخافونَ

Fill in the blank with the appropriate verb.

1. Samir _____ his two grandchildren a story from his school days.

    a. visits   b. tells   c. reads

2. That day _____ a rainy and sad day.

    a. was   b. would be   c. is

3. The air _____ clouds up.

    a. raises   b. throws   c. goes

4. Samir's mother _____ to tell funny stories to her son.

    a. heard   b. tried   c. said

5. Samir _____ his coat and hat on the bus.

    a. carried   b. took   c. took off

6. The two boys _____ on the sofa in the parlor.

    a. are sleeping   b. are lying down   c. are sitting

7. The students _____ from the Arabic language teacher.

    a. like   b. is afraid.   c. are afraid

8. أمينٌ _____ مَقْعَدِهِ وَهُوَ يَبْكي.
   أ. سافَرَ إلى   ب. عادَ إلى   ج. وَصَلَ مِن

9. _____ المُعَلِّمَةُ سَميرًا وَقالَتْ لَهُ: "اُكْتُبِ الكَلِماتِ مِنْ فَضْلِكَ."
   أ. ضَحِكَتِ   ب. نادَتِ   ج. نَظَرَتِ

10. _____ الجَدُّ القِصَّةَ عَنْ ذَلِكَ اليَوْمِ المُمْطِرِ.
    أ. يَرْوي   ب. يَسْتَمِعُ   ج. يَقْرَأُ

11. زَوْجُ سُعادَ _____ السَّريرِ كُلَّ اليَوْمِ.
    أ. يَأْكُلُ في   ب. يَسْتَلْقي عَلى   ج. يَجْلِسُ

12. "ما رَأْيُكَ في أنْ _____ قِطْعَةَ القُماشِ إلى سُعادَ يا زَوْجي؟"
    أ. تَحْمِلَ   ب. تَذْهَبَ   ج. تَأْخُذَ

13. "سُعادُ لا تَأْخُذُ مالًا لَكِنّي سَوْفَ _____ المالِ."
    أ. أُعْطيها مِنَ   ب. أُساعِدُها بِ   ج. أُعْطيها إلى

14. الوَلَدانِ يُريدانِ أنْ _____ كُلَّ شَيْءٍ عَنْ جَدِّهِما.
    أ. يَعْرِفا   ب. يَقولا   ج. يَسْمَعا

8. Amin _____ his seat crying.

    a. traveled to   b. returned to   c. arrived from

9. The teacher _____ Samir, and told him, "Write the words, please."

    a. laughed   b. called   c. looked

10. The grandfather _____ the story about that rainy day.

    a. tells   b. listens to   c. is reading

11. Souad's husband _____ the bed all day.

    a. eats in   b. lies on   c. sits

12. "What do you think of _____ the piece of cloth to Souad, my husband?"

    a. carrying   b. going   c. taking

13. "Souad does not take money, but I will _____ the money."

    a. give it from   b. help her with   c. give it to

14. The boys want to _____ everything about their grandfather.

    a. know   b. say   c. hear

15. كانَ الجَدُّ _____ البَرْدِ في المَدْرَسَةِ.
أ. شَعَرَ   ب. يَشْعُرُ بِ   ج. يَخافُ مِنَ

16. كُلُّهُم _____ لِأَنَّ سعادَ امْرَأَةٌ مُضْحِكَةٌ.
أ. ضَحِكوا   ب. جَلَسوا   ج. أَخَذوا

17. _____ الوَلَدانِ كَثيرًا كَثيرًا.
أ. ضَحِكَ   ب. أَكَلَ   ج. رَقَصَ

18. رَبَّةُ البَيْتِ _____ بِأُسْرَتِها: تَطْبُخُ وَتَغْسِلُ وَتُدَرِّسُ الأَوْلادَ.
أ. تَعْتَني   ب. تُساعِدُ   ج. تَأْخُذُ

19. أُمُّ عادِلٍ _____ أَكْوابَ الكاكاوِ بِالحَليبِ لِعَمِّها وَلِوَلَدَيْها.
أ. فَعَلَتْ   ب. قَدَّمَتْ   ج. شَرِيَتْ

20. سَوْفَ _____ والِدُ عادِلٍ اللَّوْحَةَ على جِدارِ غُرْفَةِ الجُلوسِ.
أ. يُعَلِّقُ   ب. يَسْتَلْقي   ج. يَرْمي

21. خَرَجَتْ أُمُّ سَميرٍ مِنَ البَهْوِ وَ _____ إِلى غُرْفَةِ الجُلوسِ.
أ. سارَتْ   ب. نامَتْ   ج. خَرَجَتْ

15. Grandpa _____ cold at school.

    a. feels   b. used to feel   c. is afraid of

16. They all _____ because Souad is a funny woman.

    a. laughed   b. sat   c. took

17. The two boys _____ a lot.

    a. laughed   b. ate   c. danced

18. A housewife _____ her family: she cooks, washes, and teaches the children.

    a. takes care of   b. helps   c. takes

19. Adel's mother _____ cups of cocoa with milk to her father-in-law and two sons.

    a. did   b. offered   c. drank

20. Adel's father will _____ the painting on the living room wall.

    a. hang   b. lie down   c. throw

21. Umm Samir got out of the parlor and _____ into the living room.

    a. walked   b. slept   c. got out

22. قالَ سَميرٌ لِأُمِّهِ إنَّ سُعادَ يَداها ـــــــــ.

أ. تَبْرُدانِ   ب. تُخَيِّطانِ   ج. تَرْجُفانِ

23. "يا عادِلُ، ـــــــــ إلى المَطْبَخِ لِتُساعِدَني!" قالَتْ أُمُّ عادِلٍ.

أ. اِذْهَبْ   ب. أخْرُجْ   ج. تَفَضَّلْ

22. Samir told his mother that Souad's hands _____.

   a. feel cold   b. sew   c. shake

23. "Oh Adel, _____ to the kitchen to help me!" said Adel's mother.

   a. go   b. get out   c. come

اِمْلَأِ الفَراغَ بِالعِبارَةِ المُناسِبَةِ.

1. كانَ ذَلِكَ اليَوْمُ يَوْمًا _____ وَفيهِ ريحٌ شَديدَةٌ.

   أ. جَميلًا   ب. مُمْطِرًا   ج. قَصيرًا

2. هَذا يَوْمٌ _____ وَحَزينٌ.

   أ. رَماديٌّ   ب. نَشيطٌ   ج. هَواءٌ

3. أُمُّ سَميرٍ تَقِفُ _____ في الشّارِعِ.

   أ. أمامَهُ   ب. بِجانِبِهِ   ج. عَلى يَسارِهِ

4. أُمُّ سَميرٍ تَلْبَسُ _____ .

   أ. رِداءً مِنَ الصّوفِ   ب. قُبَّعَةً كَبيرَةً   ج. قُبَّعَةً مِنَ الصّوفِ

5. قالَ سَميرٌ "صَباحُ الخَيْرِ" لِسائِقِ الباصِ لَكِنْ _____ .

   أ. بِسُرورٍ   ب. بِخَوْفٍ   ج. بِخَجَلٍ

6. مُعَلِّمَةُ سَميرٍ كانَتْ _____ .

   أ. تَقولُ النُّكَتَ   ب. تَقولُ صَباحَ الخَيْرِ   ج. تَغْضَبُ

7. كَتَبَ أمينٌ الكَلِماتِ لَكِنْ كانَ عِنْدَهُ _____ .

   أ. خَطٌّ جَميلٌ   ب. أخْطاءٌ   ج. دَفْتَرٌ مُرَتَّبٌ

Fill in the blank with the appropriate phrase.

1. That day was a _____ day with strong wind.

    a. nice   b. rainy   c. short

2. This is _____ and sad day.

    a. a gray   b. an energetic   c. air

3. Samir's mother is standing _____ on the street.

    a. in front of him   b. next to him   c. on his left

4. Samir's mother wears _____.

    a. A wool robe   b. a big hat   c. a wool hat

5. Samir said "good morning" to the bus driver, but _____.

    a. with pleasure   b. fearfully   c. shyly

6. Samir's teacher used to _____.

    a. tell jokes   b. say good morning   c. get angry

7. Amin wrote the words but had _____.

    a. beautiful handwriting   b. errors   c. a tidy book

8. سَميرٌ كانَ تِلْميذًا _____.

   أ. مُجْتَهِدًا   ب. كَسولًا   ج. خائِفًا

9. سُعادُ كانَتْ في _____ مِنْ عُمْرِها.

   أ. الخَمْسينِيّاتِ   ب. السِّتّينِيّاتِ   ج. الثَّلاثينِيّاتِ

10. عَلى الطّاوِلَةِ الصَّغيرَةِ قُرْبَ السَّريرِ كانَ هُناكَ _____.

    أ. زَوْجُ سُعاد   ب. حَلْوَياتٌ عَرَبِيَّةٌ   ج. عُلَبُ الدَّواءِ

11. أَخَذَ أَبو سَميرٍ _____ إلى ابْنَةِ عَمَّتِهِ.

    أ. قِطْعَةً مِنَ القُماشِ   ب. حَلْوَياتٍ عَرَبِيَّةً   ج. عادِلًا

12. _____ أَنْ تَذْهَبَ إلى سُعادَ في نِهايَةِ الأُسْبوعِ؟

    أ. لِماذا   ب. ما رَأْيُكَ في   ج. مَتى

13. زَوْجُ سُعادَ _____ وَصِحَّتُهُ _____.

    أ. موْجوعٌ / جَيِّدَةٌ   ب. مَريضٌ / سَيِّئَةٌ   ج. مَريضٌ / مُمْتازَةٌ

14. اِسْتَلْقى عادِلٌ عَلى الأَريكَةِ وَوَضَعَ رَأْسَهُ _____.

    أ. عَلى جَدِّهِ   ب. عَلى رَأْسِ جَدِّهِ   ج. عَلى صَدْرِ جَدِّهِ

8. Samir was a _____ student.

   a. diligent   b. lazy   c. frightened

9. Souad was in her _____.

   a. fifties   b. sixties   c. thirties

10. On the little table near the bed was/were _____.

    a. Souad's husband.   b. Arabic sweets   c. medicine boxes

11. Abu Samir took _____ to his cousin.

    a. a piece of cloth   b. Arabic sweets   c. Adel

12. _____ to Souad's at the weekend?

    a. Why do you go
    b. How about you go
    c. When will you go

13. Souad's husband _____, and his health _____.

    a. has pain / is good
    b. is sick / is bad
    c. is sick / is excellent

14. Adel lay down on the sofa and laid his head _____.

    a. on his grandfather
    b. on his grandfather's head
    c. on his grandfather's chest

15. "_____، أَكْمِلِ القِصَّةَ يا جَدّي."

أ. لَوْ سَمَحْتَ   ب. قِصَّتُكَ طَويلَةٌ   ج. ما رَأْيُكَ

16. أُمُّ سَميرٍ تُحِبُّ _____ سُعادَ في الخِياطَةِ.

أ. السَّيِّدَة   ب. الخَيّاطَة   ج. ذَوْق

17. "_____ يا مايا؟ هَلِ الخَيّاطَةُ ذَكِيَّةٌ؟"

أ. ما رَأْيُكِ   ب. نَعَمْ   ج. وَأَنْتِ

18. قَدَّمَتْ أُمُّ عادِلٍ الأَكْوابَ لِسَميرٍ وَلِوَلَدَيها وَقالَتْ : "_____!"

أ. شُكْرًا   ب. بِالهَناءِ والشِّفاءِ   ج. مَعَ السَّلامَةِ

19. سَميرٌ قالَ لِأُمِّهِ : "_____، لا أُحِبُّ لَوْنَ البِنْطالِ!"

أ. في الحَقيقَةِ   ب. أَظُنُّ   ج. الكُلُّ

20. لا شَكَّ في أَنَّ _____ سُعادَ جَميلٌ جِدًّا.

أ. ذَوْقَ   ب. زَوْجَ   ج. شَعَرَ

21. "_____ يا سُعادَ وَأَطالَ اللهُ عُمَرِكِ"، قالَتْ أُمُّ سَميرٍ.

أ. مَعَ السَّلامَةِ   ب. سَلامٌ   ج. سَلِمَتْ يَداكِ

15. "_____, go on with the story, Grandpa."

    a. Please   b. Your story is long   c. What's your opinion

16. Samir's mother loves _____ in sewing.

    a. Mrs. Souad.   B. the seamstress   c. Souad's taste

17. "_____, Maya? Is the seamstress clever?"

    a. What do you think   b. Is   c. And you

18. Umm Adel gave the cups to Samir and her two sons and said, "_____!"

    a. Thanks   b. Bon appetit   c. Good-bye

19. Samir told his mother, "_____, I don't like the color of the trousers!"

    a. In fact   b. I think   c. Everyone

20. Undoubtedly, Souad has very good _____.

    a. taste   b. husband   c. hair

21. "_____ Souad, and may God prolong your life," Umm Samir said.

    a. Goodbye   b. Peace   c. Thank you

الإجاباتُ

إِجاباتُ أَسْئِلَةِ الفَهْمِ

1. كانَ سَميرٌ في الصَّفِّ الثّالِثِ الإِبْتِدائِيِّ.

2. دَرَسَ سَميرٌ في مَدْرَسَةٍ لِلرُّهْبانِ في وَسَطِ مَدينَةِ بَيْروتَ.

3. في ذَلِكَ اليَوْمِ مِنْ أَيّامِ شَهْرِ يَنايِرَ كانَ الجَوُّ بارِدًا وَمُمْطِرًا وَفيهِ ريحٌ شَديدَةٌ.

4. لا. في ذَلِكَ اليَوْمِ، كانَ سَميرٌ حَزينًا.

5. كُلَّ يَوْمٍ يَنْتَظِرُ سَميرٌ الباصَ في الشّارِعِ.

6. لا، في ذَلِكَ اليَوْمِ ما كانَ سَميرٌ وَحْدَهُ في الشّارِعِ يَنْتَظِرُ باصَ المَدْرَسَةِ. كانَتْ أُمُّهُ مَعَهُ.

7. لَبِسَ سَميرٌ مِعْطَفًا وَوَضَعَ قُبَّعَةً لِأَنَّ الجَوَّ كانَ بارِدًا.

8. في الباصِ جَلَسَ سَميرٌ عَلى المَقْعَدِ الأخيرِ.

9. كانَ سَميرٌ مِثْلَ شَجَرَةٍ لِأَنَّ بِنْطالَهُ لَوْنُهُ بُنِّيٌّ وَكَنْزَتُهُ خَضْراءُ.

Answer Key

Comprehension Questions

1. Samir was in the third grade of elementary school.
2. Samir went to a school run by monks and located in downtown Beirut.
3. On that January day, the weather was cold, rainy, and very windy.
4. No, he wasn't. On that day, Samir was sad.
5. Every day, Samir waits for the bus on the street.
6. No, he wasn't waiting for the bus alone. His mother was standing next to him.
7. Sami wore a coat and a hat because the weather was cold.
8. On the bus, Samir sat in the back seat.
9. Samir looked like a tree because his trousers were brown and his sweater green.

10. سَميرٌ وَحَفيداهُ كانا يَجْلِسانِ عَلى الأَريكَةِ الكَبيرَةِ في البَهْوِ.

11. عادِلٌ عُمْرُهُ ثَماني سَنَواتٍ وَشَهْرانِ وَمايا عُمْرُها سِتُّ سَنَواتٍ وَسَبْعَةُ أَشْهُرٍ.

12. التَّلميذُ أَمينٌ هُوَ تِلْميذٌ نَشيطٌ وَدائِمًا يَفْعَلُ كُلَّ واجِباتِهِ. دَفْتَرُهُ مُرَتَّبٌ وَخَطُّهُ جَميلٌ.

13. كانَتْ مُعَلِّمَةُ اللُّغَةِ العَرَبِيَّةِ لَطيفَةً جِدًّا مَعَ الأَوْلادِ. وَكانَتْ جَميلَةً جِدًّا. عَيْناها خَضْراوانِ، وَفَمُها زُهْرِيٌّ، وَشَعْرُها أَسْوَدُ وَأَمْلَسُ. تَشْرَحُ دُروسًا سَهْلَةً وَتَقولُ النُّكَتَ.

14. نَعَمْ، مايا تُحِبُّ مُعَلِّمَةَ اللُّغَةِ العَرَبِيَّةِ في مَدْرَسَتِها.

10. Samir and his two grandchildren were sitting on the large sofa in the parlor.

11. Adel is eight years and two months old, and Maya is six years and seven months old.

12. Amin is a smart student and always does all his homework. His notebook is neat, and his handwriting is very beautiful.

13. The Arabic language teacher was very nice to the students. She was very pretty; her eyes were green, her mouth pink, and her hair black and straight. She used to explain easy lessons and tell jokes.

14. Yes, she likes the Arabic teacher in her school.

15. قالَتْ: " التّاءُ في الكَلِمَةِ الصِّفةِ بَرْدانَةٌ هِيَ حَقًّا بَرْدانَةٌ. لِماذا؟ لِأَنَّ يَدَها اليُسْرى لا تَتْرُكُ يَدَها اليُمْنى. لَكِنِ التّاءُ في الكَلِمَةِ الفِعْلِ لَيْسَتْ بَرْدانَةً."

16. عادَ أمينٌ إلى مَقْعَدِهِ وَهُوَ يَبْكي لِأَنَّهُ كَتَبَ الكَلِمَةَ الصِّفَةَ خَطَأً، وَكَتَبَ فِعْلًا مِنَ الفِعْلَيْنِ خَطَأً أَيْضًا.

17. سُعادُ تَعْمَلُ خَيّاطَةً.

18. عَلى الطّاوِلَةِ الصَّغيرَةِ بِالقُرْبِ مِنْ سَريرِ زَوْجِ سُعادٍ كانَ هُناكَ الكَثيرُ مِنْ عُلَبِ الدَّواءِ.

19. لا، أُمُّ سَميرٍ ما اشْتَرَتْ قِطْعَةَ القُماشِ. قِطْعَةُ القُماشِ هَدِيَّةٌ مِنْ زَوْجِها في عيدِ ميلادِها قَبْلَ سَنَتَيْنِ.

20. أُمُّ سَميرٍ تُريدُ مِنْ سُعادَ أَنْ تَفْعَلَ بِنْطالًا لِسَميرٍ.

15. The teacher said, "The ta' in the adjective word 'cold' is really cold. Why? Because her left hand does not leave its right hand. But the ta' in the verb is not cold."
16. Amin returned to his seat crying because he wrote the adjective word incorrectly and wrote one of the two verbs incorrectly, as well.
17. Souad is a seamstress.
18. On the little table near the bed of Souad's husband were many medicine boxes.
19. No, she didn't. The piece of cloth was her husband's gift for her birthday two years ago.
20. Samir's mother wants Souad to make trousers for Samir with the piece of cloth.

21. أبو سَميرٍ أحَبَّ فِكْرَةَ زَوْجَتِهِ وَقالَ إنَّ سُعاد لا تَأْخُذُ مالًا مِنْهُ لَكِنَّهُ سَيُساعِدُها بِالمالِ.

22. كانَتْ سُعادُ في حاجةٍ إلى الكَثيرِ مِنَ المالِ لِأنَّها تُريدُ أنْ تَشْتَرِيَ الأدْوِيةَ لِزَوْجِها.

23. ذَهَبَ سَميرٌ وَأبوهُ إلى الخَيّاطةِ في يَوْمِ السَّبْتِ.

24. كانَ البِنْطالُ جاهِزًا في يَوْمِ الاِثْنَيْنِ.

25. مايا تَعْرِفُ أنَّ سُعادَ امْرَأةٌ ذَكِيَّةٌ لِأنَّ سُعادَ مُضْحِكَةٌ.

26. زَبوناتُ سُعادَ مِنْ بَيْروتَ وَمِنْ مُدُنٍ أُخرى. عِنْدَها زَبوناتٌ مِنَ القُرى أيْضًا.

27. سُعادُ تُحَضِّرُ الحَلْوَياتِ العَرَبِيَّةَ مِثْلَ الأرُزِّ بِالحَليبِ والمُهَلَّبِيَّةِ والمَعْمولِ وَلَيالي لُبْنانَ والبَقْلاوةِ.

28. لا، ما كانَتْ أُمُّ سَميرٍ تَعْمَلُ. كانَتْ رَبَّةَ بَيْتٍ.

21. Abu Samir liked his wife's idea and said that Souad would not take money from him, but he would help her with the money.
22. Souad needed a lot of money because she wanted to buy medicine for her husband.
23. Samir and his father went to the seamstress on a Saturday.
24. The trousers were ready on Monday.
25. Maya knows that Souad is an intelligent woman because Souad is funny.
26. Souad's customers are from Beirut and other cities. She also has customers from villages.
27. Souad prepares Arabic sweets such as roz bihalib (rice pudding), mouhallabiah (pudding), maamoul, Layali Lubnan (Lebanese nights), and baklava.
28. No, Samir's mother didn't have a job. She was a housewife.

29. عادِلٌ رَسَمَ لَوْحَةً كَبِيرَةً.

30. كانَتْ مايا تَذْهَبُ إلى مَدْرَسَةٍ لِلرَّقْصِ كُلَّ يَوْمِ ثُلاثاءٍ.

31. لا يُحِبُّ سَميرٌ البِنْطالَ لِأنَّ لَوْنَهُ بُنِّيٌّ وَفي رَأيِهِ هذا لَوْنٌ لِلكِبارِ.

32. لا، سَميرٌ ما قالَ إنَّ سُعادَ خَيّاطَةٌ مُمْتازَةٌ. هُوَ قالَ إنَّ سُعادَ كانَتْ خَيّاطَةً مُمْتازَةً لَكِنَّها الآنَ كَبيرَةٌ في السِّنِّ.

33. يَقولُ سَميرٌ إنَّ أُمَّهُ كانَتْ قاسِيَةً قَليلًا وَلَيسَ كَثيرًا لِأنَّ الأُمَّ دائِمًا تُريدُ الشَّيْءَ الجَميلَ لِأبْنائِها.

34. ضَحِكَ الثَّلاثَةُ وَأصْبَحَ وَجْهُ عادِلٍ أحْمَرَ قَبْلَ نِهايَةِ القِصَّةِ لِأنَّهُ قالَ إنَّ أُمَّهُ لا تَسْتَخْدِمُ فِعْلَ الأمْرِ مَعَهُ وَمَعَ أُخْتِهِ لَكِنَّها قالَتْ لَهُ: " تَفَضَّلْ إلى المَطْبَخِ الآنَ وَبِسُرْعَةٍ. ساعِدْني لِنَأخُذَ الصُّحونَ إلى مائِدَةِ غُرْفَةِ الطَّعامِ."

35. تَحْتَ كَنْزَةِ الصّوفِ الخَضْراءِ لَبِسَ سَميرٌ كَنْزَةً ثانِيَةً.

29. Adel drew a big painting.

30. Every Tuesday, Maya went to a dance school.

31. Samir does not like the trousers because they are brown, a color for adults.

32. No, Samir didn't say that Souad is an excellent seamstress. He said that Souad used to be an excellent seamstress, but she is very old now.

33. Samir says that his mother was a little harsh, and not very harsh because a mother always wants something beautiful for her children.

34. The three of them laughed, and Adel's face turned red before the end of the story because he said that his mother does not use the imperative verb with him and his sister, but she called out to him to go to the kitchen on the spot to help her take the plates to the dining-room table.

35. Under the green wool sweater, Samir wore a second sweater.

صَحيحٌ أَمْ خَطَأٌ أَمْ لا نَعْرِفُ؟

1. <u>خَطَأ.</u> كانَتْ مَدْرَسَةُ سَميرٍ في وَسَطِ مَدينَةِ بَيْروتَ.
2. <u>خَطَأ.</u> كُلَّ يَوْمٍ يَنْتَظِرُ سَميرٌ باصَ المَدْرَسَةِ وَحْدَهُ.
3. صَحيحٌ.
4. <u>خَطَأ.</u> جَلَسَ سَميرٌ في المَقْعَدِ الخَلْفيِّ. هُناك لا يَجْلِسُ التَّلاميذُ.
5. <u>صَحيحٌ.</u>
6. <u>لا نَعْرِفُ.</u>
7. <u>خَطَأ.</u> مُعَلِّمَةُ اللُّغَةِ العَرَبيَّةِ في مَدْرَسَةِ سَميرٍ كانَتْ لَطيفَةً.
8. <u>صَحيحٌ.</u>
9. <u>خَطَأ.</u> كَتَبَ أمينٌ كَلِمَتَيْنِ خَطَأً.
10. <u>لا نَعْرِفُ.</u>
11. <u>لا نَعْرِفُ.</u>

True, False, or Unknown?

1. <u>False.</u> Samir's school was in downtown Beirut.
2. <u>False.</u> Every day, Samir waits for the school bus alone.
3. <u>True.</u>
4. <u>False.</u> Samir sat in the back seat. Students do not sit there.
5. <u>True.</u>
6. <u>We do not know.</u>
7. <u>False.</u> The Arabic language teacher at Samir's school was nice to students.
8. <u>True.</u>
9. <u>False.</u> Amin wrote two words wrong.
10. <u>We do not know.</u>
11. <u>We do not know.</u>

12. <u>خَطَأ</u>. أبو سَميرٍ اِشْتَرى لِزَوْجَتِهِ قِطْعَةَ قُماشٍ لَوْنُها بُنِّيٌّ.

13. <u>خَطَأ</u>. سُعادُ اِبْنَةُ عَمَّةِ سَميرٍ وَهِيَ تَسْكُنُ في بَيْروتَ.

14. <u>لا نَعْرِفُ.</u>

15. <u>لا نَعْرِفُ.</u>

16. <u>صَحيحٌ.</u>

17. <u>خَطَأ</u>. كانَ سَميرٌ يَزورُ سُعادَ مَعَ أبيهِ أوْ مَعَ أُمِّهِ أوْ مَعَ أبيهِ وَأُمِّهِ.

18. <u>صَحيحٌ.</u>

19. <u>صَحيحٌ.</u>

20. <u>خَطَأ</u>. سَميرٌ هوَ والِدُ أبي عادِلٍ.

12. <u>False.</u> Abu Samir bought a piece of brown cloth for his wife.
13. <u>False.</u> Souad is Samir's cousin, and she lives in Beirut.
14. <u>We do not know.</u>
15. <u>We do not know.</u>
16. <u>True.</u>
17. <u>False.</u> Samir used to visit Souad with his father, with his mother, or with his father and mother.
18. <u>True.</u>
19. <u>True.</u>
20. <u>False.</u> Samir is the father of Adel's father.

اِمْلَأِ الفَراغَ بِالفِعْلِ المُناسِبِ.

1. ب. يَرْوي
2. أ. كانَ
3. أ. يَرْفَعُ
4. ب. حاوَلَتْ
5. ج. خَلَعَ
6. ج. يَجْلِسانِ
7. ج. يَخافونَ
8. ب. عادَ إلى
9. ب. نادَتْ
10. أ. يَرْوي
11. ب. يَسْتَلْقي عَلى
12. ج. تَأْخُذَ
13. ب. أُساعِدُها بِـ
14. أ. يَعْرِفا
15. ب. يَشْعُرُ بِـ
16. أ. ضَحِكوا
17. أ. ضَحِكَ
18. أ. تَعْتَني
19. ب. قَدَّمَتْ
20. أ. يُعَلِّقُ
21. أ. سارَتْ
22. ج. تَرْجُفانِ
23. ج. تُفَضِّلْ

Fill in the blank with the appropriate verb.

1. b. tells
2. a. was
3. a. raises
4. b. tried
5. c. took off
6. c. are sitting
7. c. are afraid
8. b. returned to
9. b. called
10. a. tells
11. b. lies on
12. c. taking
13. b. help her with
14. a. know
15. b. used to feel
16. a. laughed
17. a. laughed
18. a. takes care of
19. b. offered
20. a. hang
21. a. walked
22. c. shake
23. c. come

اِمْلَأِ الفَراغَ بِالعِبارَةِ المُناسِبَةِ.

1. ب. مُمْطِرًا
2. أ. رَماديٌّ
3. ب. بِجانِبِهِ
4. أ. رِداءً مِنَ الصّوفِ
5. ج. بِخَجَلٍ
6. أ. تَقولُ النُّكَتَ
7. ب. أَخْطاءٌ
8. أ. مُجْتَهِدًا
9. ب. السِّتّينيّاتِ
10. ج. عُلَبُ الدَّواءِ
11. أ. قِطْعَةً مِنْ القُماشِ
12. ب. ما رَأْيُكَ في
13. ب. مَريضٌ / سَيِّئَةٌ
14. ج. عَلى صَدْرِ جَدِّهِ
15. أ. لَوْ سَمَحْتَ
16. ج. ذَوْقَ
17. أ. ما رَأْيُكِ
18. ب. بِالهَناءِ والشِّفاءِ
19. أ. في الحَقيقَةِ
20. أ. ذَوْقَ
21. ج. سَلِمَتْ يَداكِ

Fill in the blank with the appropriate phrase.

1. b. rainy
2. a. a gray
3. b. next to him
4. a. a wool robe
5. c. shyly
6. a. tell jokes
7. b. errors
8. a. diligent
9. b. sixties
10. c. medicine boxes
11. a. a piece of cloth
12. b. How about you go
13. b. is sick/ is bad
14. c. on his grandfather's chest
15. a. Please
16. c. Souad's taste
17. a. What do you think
18. b. Bon appetit
19. a. In fact
20. a. taste
21. c. Thank you

Glossary

Nouns

Irregular plural nouns are shown in parentheses. ج = pl. (plural)

sofa	أَرِيكَةٌ (ج. أَرائِكُ)
dictation, spelling	إِمْلاءٌ
composition	إِنْشاءٌ (ج. إِنْشاءاتٌ)
the imperative (in grammar)	الأَمْرُ
cookies	بَسْكَوِيتٌ
trousers, pants	بِنْطالٌ (ج. بَناطيلُ)
parlor (formal sitting room for entertaining guests)	بَهْوٌ (ج. أَبْهاءٌ)
Beirut	بَيْروتُ
aunt	تانْتْ
heating	تَدْفِئَةٌ
neighbor	جارٌ (ةٌ) (ج. جيرانٌ / جاراتٌ)
grief	حُزْنٌ (ج. أَحْزانٌ)
sweet (pastry, confection)	حَلْوى (ج. حَلْوَياتٌ)
neighborhood	حَيٌّ (ج. أَحْياءٌ)

embarrassment	خَجَلٌ
handwriting	خَطٌّ (ج. خُطوطٌ)
seamstress	خَيّاطَةٌ
sewing	خِياطَةٌ
tear, teardrop	دَمْعَةٌ (ج. دُموعٌ)
taste	ذَوْقٌ (ج. أَذْواقٌ)
opinion	رَأْيٌ (ج. آراءٌ)
monk	راهِبٌ (ج. رُهْبانٌ)
robe	رِداءٌ (ج. رِداءاتٌ)
client	زَبونٌ (ـةٌ) (ج. زَبائِنُ / زَبوناتٌ)
knife	سِكّينٌ (ج. سَكاكينُ)
lady	سَيِّدَةٌ
chest	صَدْرٌ (ج. صُدورٌ)
adjective	صِفَةٌ
voice	صَوْتٌ (ج. أَصْواتٌ)
expression	عِبارَةٌ
father-in-law	عَمٌّ (ج. أَعْمامٌ)
dining room	غُرْفَةُ طعامٍ (ج. غُرَفُ طعامٍ)

cloud	غَيْمَةٌ (ج. غُيومٌ)
season	فَصْلٌ (ج. فُصولٌ)
verb	فِعْلٌ (ج. أَفعالٌ)
hat	قُبَّعَةٌ
story	قِصَّةٌ (ج. قِصَصٌ)
cloth	قُماشٌ (ج. أَقْمِشَةٌ)
cocoa	كاكاوٌ
Lebanon	لُبْنانُ
store	مَحَلٌّ (ج. مَحالُّ؛ مَحَلّاتٌ)
toothpaste	مَعْجونُ أَسْنانٍ (ج. مَعاجينُ أَسْنانٍ)
bench	مَقْعَدٌ (ج. مَقاعِدُ)
playground	مَلْعَبٌ (ج. مَلاعِبُ)
joke	نُكْتَةٌ (ج. نُكَتٌ)
rose	وَرْدَةٌ (ج. وَرْدٌ / وَرْداتٌ)
downtown	وَسَطُ المَدينَةِ
January	يَنايِرُ

Adjectives

Feminine adjective forms are shown in parentheses.

straight; smooth	أَمْلَسُ (مَلْساءُ)
elegant	أَنيقٌ (ـَةٌ)
elementary	اِبْتِدائِيٌّ (ـَةٌ)
cold	بارِدٌ (ةٌ)
Beiruti	بَيْروتِيٌّ (ـَةٌ)
intelligent, smart	ذَكِيٌّ (ـَةٌ)
harsh	قاسٍ (قاسِيَةٌ)
generous	كَريمٌ (ـَةٌ)
diligent	مُجْتَهِدٌ (ةٌ)
curly	مُجَعَّدٌ (ةٌ)
neat	مُرَتَّبٌ (ـَةٌ)
delighted	مَسْرورٌ (ةٌ)
poor, pitiable	مِسْكينٌ (ـَةٌ)
in pain	مَوْجوعٌ (ـَةٌ)
skinny	نَحيلٌ (ـَةٌ)

Verbs

Verbs are given in the third-person singular forms of the perfect tense followed by the imperfect, which can be used to conjugate for other persons.

to reply	أجابَ - يُجيبُ
to prolong	أطالَ - يُطيلُ
to continue	أكْمَلَ - يُكْمِلُ
to smile	اِبْتَسَمَ - يَبْتَسِمُ
to care	اِعْتَنى - يَعْتَني بِـ
to wait	اِنْتَظَرَ - يَنْتَظِرُ
to continue	تابَعَ - يُتابِعُ
to pick up	حَمَلَ - يَحْمِلُ
to take off	خَلَعَ - يَخْلَعُ
to wish	رَجا - يَرْجو مِنْ
to shake	رَجَفَ - يَرجُفُ
to feel cold	شَعَرَ - يَشْعُرُ بِالبَرْدِ
to hug	عانَقَ - يُعانِقُ
to hang	عَلَّقَ - يُعَلِّقُ
to mean	عَنى - يَعْني

to lay	وَضَعَ - يَضَعُ

Other

right?; won't you?, isn't it?, etc.	أَلَيْسَ كَذَلِكَ؟
right away	الآنَ وَبِسُرْعَةٍ
praise be to God	الحَمْدُ لِلّهِ
shyly	بِخَجَلٍ
loudly	بِصَوْتٍ مُرْتَفِعٍ
soon, shortly	بَعْدَ قَلِيلٍ
May God have mercy on her	رَحِمَها اللهُ
so	فَ
in her sixties	في السِّتِّينِيّاتِ مِنْ عُمْرِها
God forbid	لا سَمَحَ اللهُ
no doubt	لا شَكَّ
neither... nor...	لا... وَلا...
similar to	مِثْلُ
come on!	هَيّا!

lingualism

Visit our website for information on current and upcoming titles, free excerpts, and language learning resources in Modern Standard Arabic, colloquial Arabic dialects, and other languages.

www.lingualism.com